CW01629445

ENGLISH CLIMATE: WARTIME STORIES

Persephone Book N° 137
Published by Persephone Books Ltd 2020
Reprinted 2022

© The Estate of Sylvia Townsend Warner

Preface © Lydia Fellgett

Endpapers taken from Sailors, a 1940–41 Calico Printers Association dress fabric. In a private collection.

Typeset in ITC Baskerville by
KSPM, Tettenhall, Wolverhampton

Printed and bound in Germany by
GGP Media GmbH, Poessneck

978 1910 263 273

Persephone Books Ltd
8 Edgar Buildings
Bath BA1 2EE
01225 425050

www.persephonebooks.co.uk

ENGLISH CLIMATE: WARTIME STORIES

by

SYLVIA TOWNSEND WARNER

with a new preface by

LYDIA FELLGETT

PERSEPHONE BOOKS
BATH

PUBLISHER'S NOTE

These twenty-two stories are reprinted in chronological order. Nine of the 1940–43 stories appeared in *A Garland of Straw and Other Stories* in 1943 (seven were first in *The New Yorker*); eight of the 1943–46 stories appeared in *The Museum of Cheats and Other Stories* in 1947 (six were first in *The New Yorker*); four stories ('Scorched Earth Policy', 'The Family Revived', 'England, Home and Beauty' and 'It's What We're Here For') were published in *The New Yorker* in 1942–43 and have not been reprinted since; 'My Shirt is in Mexico' was originally published in *The New Yorker* as 'The Shirt in Mexico' and 'From Above' as 'Dropped from Heaven'; 'Arsace, Il Faut Partir' was published in *English Story: Sixth Series* in 1945 and has not been reprinted since.

CONTENTS

PREFACE

The publication of these short stories comes just over eighty years since the beginning of the Second World War, a war which Sylvia Townsend Warner knew would produce great works of art that would attempt, and inevitably often fail, to understand its full meaning. As she wrote in 1940 in a letter to a friend: 'For all its violence, war is papery-thin compared to a garden with apple trees and cabbages in it. Even when it's forced down one's throat, one can't swallow it.'[1] These twenty-one stories were her attempt to do just that: collected together for the first time, they are arranged in chronological order and show a writer seeking to understand what life was like in Britain at war. She worked quickly, without the haze of nostalgia, and (unlike her novels which moved between the centuries) they were always contemporary, reflecting the texture of what was happening at that moment in time. Her wartime stories therefore, collected here as *English Climate* epitomise what the historian Juliet Gardiner calls 'fingertip history'; a telling of an age that is so close that you can still just about touch it. For some time ignored, these short stories now take their rightful place amongst the best of Sylvia Townsend Warner's work.

Almost all are set in the market towns and villages of Southern England's countryside, with a few recurring characters providing snapshots of communities of women throughout the war. Most of them appeared for the first time in *The New Yorker:* between 1936 and 1977 over a hundred and fifty were published there. Occasionally a British reader senses a direct explanation of some quirk of specifically English culture for her American audience but, generally, the appeal they held for the *New Yorker* readership then carries over to the appeal they hold for a twenty-first century Persephone reader today. Funny, brilliantly written, at times utterly heartbreaking, delightfully sharp, dry, intelligent and full of memorable characters: they are stories that strike the reader as somehow true as only the best fiction can.

It is very possible that Persephone readers have already encountered some of Sylvia Townsend Warner's work. There are countless essays and articles lamenting the demise of her reputation when, of course, compared to most other Persephone authors, she is 'famous'. She was a bestseller in her lifetime, a recognisable name on the literary prize shortlists, and something of an eccentric public intellectual. Photographs of her with her round tortoiseshell glasses, cackling mirthfully with at least one cat on her lap and ever-present cigarette in hand, are two-a-penny online. She has also been recuperated as a 'woman writer', a 'historical writer', a 'lesbian writer', a 'fantasy writer' etc. for forty years or so now. The Virago editions of her novels appeared just a few years after her death and various reprints by other publishers continue to keep much of her work in print. As with all other significant women writers of the twentieth century she has been compared to Virginia Woolf (shorthand for 'good woman writer') but, more often, her short stories in particular find her being compared to Jane Austen by readers and critics who understand them as amusing but essentially genteel sketches.

There is an element of truth to this, yet it is far too reductive and misses the quite radical unconventionality of many of her mainly female characters. She had a Sitwell-ish fondness for barmy-sounding names which reflects this: Mrs Winter of Winter's Harrow and her sister Mrs Bulteel of Mugdown St Magdalen to name but two. And, notably, the emphasis on marriage so present in Austen's writing is almost entirely absent in Warner's. That is not to say that her writing wasn't concerned with romance. In *The Summer Will Show* (1936) a separated woman, Sophia, falls in love with her husband's mistress amongst the barricades of the French Revolution. But neither the wealthy Dona Ana in *After the Death of Don Juan* (1938) nor the orphaned Sukey in *The True Heart* (1929) sit quietly at home waiting for their objects of affection to pursue them: they both bravely embark on heroic quests in order to make sure that they win the men they desire. Lolly Willowes, her most famous heroine, rejects conventional relationships altogether, leaving the family home in London to live in the countryside and become a witch.

We now recognise that is it partly *because* Sylvia Townsend Warner's writing is so difficult to categorise that it is not as widely read as it perhaps should be. The short stories collected in this volume, however, form an obvious cohesive body of work, something it is much harder to say about her novels and poetry. This is partly because they are all centred around the Second World War. They are therefore very much a companion to the other war stories published by Persephone Books. Like Mollie Panter-Downes, for example, author of *Good Evening, Mrs Craven: the Wartime Stories* (PB 8), *Minnie's Room* (PB 34) and *London War Notes* (PB 111), all of which were also originally published in the *New Yorker*, Townsend Warner's 'concentration on the personal and the particular is well suited to the magnifying lens of the short story form' (Preface to *Good Evening, Mrs Craven*[2]). Both of these writers excelled at small, everyday experiences: a woman's angry hoovering when her pride is hurt; the terror of picking up a cold at a Mothers' Union Meeting; gossiping do-gooders in a knitting circle.

The stories, too, stand alongside many others of Persephone's Second World War novels. Like Noel Streatfeild's *Saplings* (PB 16) and Barbara Noble's *Doreen* (PB 60), they are alert to the psychological impact of war on those at home, particularly children. Put simply, Warner knew that 'lack of sleep, lack of fruit and vegetables, weighs heavily on children. . .'[3] Her characters often display the eccentric heroism of Nora Ranskill (in *Miss Ranskill Comes Home*, PB 46) alongside the moral difficulties encountered by the women in *To Bed with Grand Music* (PB 86). Almost all touch on the quiet violence of life lived during wartime in original ways. In one story, for example, a family funeral is interrupted by planes overhead and the mourners are forced to leap in to the open grave with the coffin. It is perhaps this combination of eccentricity and formality that best characterises Warner's work, as well as her life: she was in some ways fiercely conservative, for example she was always a believer in excellent manners. But then in her sexuality and her politics she was a true radical – living openly with a woman as a Communist when both of those things were unheard of to most of British society. Hers was therefore an exceptional life. And yet it was also full of all the everyday dullness of a middle-class woman's existence in the middle of the twentieth century

Sylvia Nora Townsend Warner was born in 1893 in Harrow-on-the-Hill to George Townsend Warner and his young wife Nora Huddleston (who had been brought up partly in India). George was a master at Harrow School, where his grandfather, the Reverend George Townsend Warner, had also taught in the 1840s. Sylvia was educated at home, an adored only child. She was short-sighted and plain, to the disappointment of her female relatives. But she was clever and quick, much to her father's pride. She grew up amongst, but apart from, the male students at Harrow, and she discovered music at a young age. Even from those early years she had what her biographer, Claire Harman, describes as an 'aura of oddity and daring in the eyes of her own society.'[4] In 1913 she embarked on a lengthy, and very secret, affair with the (married) musicologist Dr Percy Buck.

At the age of 21, in the autumn of 1915, Sylvia responded to a notice in the newspaper about a scheme to train middle-class women in munitions-making and a few weeks later had moved to a factory in Surrey. She took with her sensible shoes and left with a heartfelt respect for the labouring classes.

When her father, who had been working for the Foreign Office, died in 1916 it, in her own words, 'mutilated' her. But it did mean the she had an annual allowance of £100 and therefore a means of independence. After the war ended she signed up to become a co-editor of the Tudor Church Music Project which offered a salary of £3 per week, enough to rent a flat in Bayswater.

The first volume appeared in 1922 and in 1923 she moved to another, nearby flat, rented from the Ecclesiastical Commission, which she shared with a black chow from her mother's kennels (animals were a huge part of her life and she often had several cats and rabbits as well as dogs as pets). She favoured living amongst vivid colours: a later house had a hot pink bathroom and terracotta and yellow walls throughout. Being in London meant that she was able to develop a crucial creative network of writers and musicians. She became a member of the Bach Choir and often ate with Old Harrovians in central London. And she began to write poetry. In 1923 she also started writing a novel that she called 'The Quick and the Dead'. It was soon abandoned in favour of a story about a contemporary witch: this would become the seed for her first novel *Lolly Willowes*.

In the autumn of 1923 David Garnett showed some of Sylvia's poems to Charles Prentice at Chatto & Windus (the volume became *The Espalier* which was published in 1925). *Lolly Willowes* had been accepted at the same time as the poems and came out in 1926. Sales were enormous. It was reprinted twice in one week in February (the book appeared in January) and had sold over 10,000 copies in the US by June of the same year. It was also nominated for the Prix Femina (which was won that year by Radclyffe Hall). A year after *Mrs Dalloway*, here was a different kind of middle-class heroine struggling, this time joyfully, with her own eroticism. Sylvia Townsend Warner was a literary hit and she was subsequently asked to contribute to *The Nation, Time and Tide* and other journals of the day.

In 1927 she finished her second novel, *Mr Fortune's Maggot,* which was again very enthusiastically received and shortlisted for the James Tait Black prize. In the same year she began a study of the writer T F (Theodore Francis) Powys; now best remembered (if at all) for the 1923 allegorical novel *Mr Weston's Good Wine*, he lived at East Chaldon in Dorset from 1904-40, making it something of a hot-spot for bookish tourists in the inter-war years. In 1930 Sylvia, on the back of a successful visit to New York, where she was feted by all the literary celebrities of the day, but disappointed by the lack of critical success of her third novel *The True Heart*, went to visit her friends the Powyses in Dorset. Here she again encountered twenty-four year-old Valentine Ackland, a tall, quiet and handsome poet. This would become the most important relationship in both of their lives and arguably the most significant lesbian relationship in the world of twentieth century British letters.

Mary Kathleen Macrory Ackland (she later chose the name Valentine) was born in 1906, daughter of Robert Craig Ackland, a West End dentist, and Ruth Macrory, the youngest daughter of a successful barrister. She grew up in Brook Street in Mayfair. Her relationship with Sylvia was not her first with a woman. In the summer of 1928, for example, Valentine had a brief affair with Dorothy Warren, owner of the Warren Gallery in Maddox Street, who was the niece of Ottoline Morrell and god-daughter of Henry James. It was around this time that 'Molly', as Valentine was known by her family, living alone in Bloomsbury, had developed a drinking habit which would secretly plague her for the rest of her life. Not that anyone could tell at the time: she was adept at hiding the day-time cocktails and the next-day hangovers. But for decades she used alcohol to hide the disappointment she felt at never becoming a first-rate poet. After Sylvia and Valentine moved in together in 1930 they spent the rest of their lives as 'wives' (they of course couldn't legally marry), moving between Essex, Norfolk and Dorset. The letters and poetry that they wrote for each other are some of the greatest pieces of romantic writing produced in the twentieth century and are a lasting testament to their deep love and devotion.

Over the course of the 1930s politics played an ever-larger role in both women's lives. Valentine's increasing concern about the rise of Fascism in Europe and indeed the fascist party in Britain saw them become members of the Communist Party of Great Britain in 1935. Both Sylvia and Valentine were attracted to the anti-fascist stance of the party: they had a natural revulsion against corruption and found some solidarity with the other communist 'outcasts'. The clear human rights crisis that was taking place in Spain emboldened the politics of many British people, propelling them to the left in the face of a right-wing military coup just across the channel. Sylvia's fifth novel, *After the Death of Don Juan* (1938), is set in late eighteenth-century Spain and was directly inspired by the month that both women spent in a Red Cross unit in Barcelona in 1936. On their return they went on writing appeals for humanitarian assistance for the people of Spain, and the stay would continue to inform their politics for years to come.

It was Jean Untermeyer, the American poet, who first suggested that Sylvia write for the *New Yorker*. Yet Sylvia was so convinced that they would turn her down that she bet Jean five pounds to that effect. She submitted 'My Mother Won the War' and it was published on 30th May 1936. She had lost her bet and had officially been admitted to the *New Yorker* fold, guaranteeing a kind of financial security unavailable to most writers. It was such a steady income that for the rest of her life she was known to refer to the *New Yorker* as 'my gentleman friend'. In Britain her new political writing was being less favourably received than her earlier work, but in America Sylvia retained a small, dedicated readership through her *New Yorker* stories, several of which were appearing each year. Sylvia and Valentine visited the US for the League of American Writers Conference in September 1939, just a few days after war was declared, being entertained by Dorothy Parker and meeting Theodore Dreiser, Thomas Mann, Lillian Hellman and the poet Elsa Gidlow. Sylvia particularly wanted to go to the *New Yorker* offices to meet her young editor William Maxwell. There was an instant connection and he became a dear and valued friend. Indeed, he tried to persuade her to stay in the US, where she would escape the war in Europe, but both women were eager to return home. They docked back in Southampton on 11th October 1939, by which time the phoney war had begun and over a million Londoners had been evacuated out to the countryside.

In 1937 Sylvia and Valentine had moved to a house in a Dorset village with a very Townsend Warner-esque name: Frome Vauchurch. It was near Maiden Newton, and cost £63.10 a year to rent, had three upstairs rooms, three downstairs rooms, a scullery and a sunroom. Because it clung so close to the river Frome, it had been partially clad in corrugated iron so, by all accounts, its great appeal lay in the views from it rather than the views of it. Both of their workrooms faced the river with its trout and moorhens and on the other side was the magnificent garden which they both spent so much of their free time tending. At the end of the war, threatened with removal, Valentine would buy the house for £2200 (borrowed from her mother and repaid at 4% interest). And later still, when she had died and Sylvia was living there on her own with the cats and the rabbits, she would maintain her strict writing schedule: waking at 6.30 and writing until 8.30, drinking black coffee and eating bread and honey. It was, in short, their home.

So this was where they spent the war, close to, and yet apart from, the main village with all the local life that Sylvia so perfectly mined for her stories. But their rural life was not cut off from the rest of the world. As well as the Baedeker raids on Bath and Exeter, we read about her receiving news about the fall of Paris, about the updates from Addis Ababa, Belgrade, Singapore, Java, Hong Kong and Burma. We know from the two women's diaries and letters that life in rural

Britain was no bucolic ideal: it was tough. The Luftwaffe was targeting the ports at nearby Portsmouth and Plymouth. Being close to the sea meant a real threat of invasion, so Sylvia and Valentine had to dig deep trenches in their gardens for safety as they listened to the bombers flying overhead night after night on their way to the docks. Much of their days were given over to doing mucky domestic jobs too: painting doors and waxing the wooden floors and whilst Valentine seems to have had lots of headaches, the diaries show her often at the sink with a pile of washing up to do. Food, of course, was scarce, although they grew vegetables in their huge garden including broccoli, green peas, onions, as well as raspberries. And they planted cutting flowers – sweet peas and hyacinths being favourites. Of course, being in the countryside did have its advantages: 'if it were not for the local ocean casting us an occasional crab, and what we rear in the garden,' Sylvia writes, 'we should be living on tinned turnips and breast of mutton.'[5]

Sylvia joined the local branch of the Women's Volunteer Service at the beginning of the war and was swiftly appointed Secretary, working two days a week at the headquarters in Colliton House in Dorchester, while Valentine worked six days a week at the Territorial Army. Sylvia's main responsibility was to organise rest centres for evacuees from the cities, co-ordinating and carrying out inspections of centres, checking supplies, rehearsing for emergencies. They also worked at the National Salvage depot, sorting through donations of clothing and books. Any especially rare volumes were stockpiled for the Blitzed Libraries scheme: an attempt to rebuild the stock of libraries that had been bombed and destroyed. Told that their house had been selected as a machine-gun post, Sylvia and Valentine attended classes in hand-grenade throwing and rifle shooting. Sylvia also gave lectures to the Army on a vast range of subjects until she was sacked for overtly left-wing views. Amongst all this she found time to edit a selection of morality tales (*The Cat's Cradle Book* 1940) and start writing *The Corner that Held Them* (1948), a novel about fourteenth century nuns which took six years to finish. It was her favourite of her novels. Her letters show her juggling domestic tasks with her attempts to finish her novel alongside her sending requests for bookseller friends to post books to prisoner of war camps. The two women would often take late-night walks where they would practise their whistle-blowing technique (quietly) in case they were called upon to rouse the village in the aftermath of an incendiary bomb falling.

Three separate evacuated families stayed with them during the course of the war. Dorchester and the surrounding villages were banned as locations for a few years because it was deemed too dangerous, but when the ban was lifted again they became 'flooded with evacuees':

> I spend day after day conferring with Public Assistance, Relieving Officers, Billetting Officers, WVS ladies; and hastening from one Rest Centre to another saying words of comfort such as soap flakes can be made out of solid soap by means of a cheese-grater, nobody need be ashamed of lice nowadays, salads will not be appreciated without vinegar, Londoners seldom like

> porridge, pubs open at six, nettle stings are not the same as nettle-rash, fish and chips will come out in a van, lost prams shall be traced, those are *our* planes, Londoners can't be expected to go to bed before eleven, the old lady will probably leave off crying if you can get her to take her shoes off, cows don't bite, have you put up a washing-line, nursing mothers must have early morning tea, buses run on Wednesdays and Saturdays, etc. . .[6]

And still they stayed as sociable as ever. Nancy Cunard, one of the rare female friends that the women shared, would often come to visit, staying at the village pub so as not to impose. Sylvia's close relationship with William Maxwell continued: she once wrote affectionately to him, 'I think of you so often. You might turn round in the street and see my anxious ghost looking after you.'[7] But during these war years she often didn't know whether the stories she sent him had been included in the magazine or rejected, sometimes not receiving cheques for the ones that were printed and certainly not seeing the final versions in the print edition of the magazine. As she wrote to a friend on 27th February 1941:

> It is all very well for you to read my stories in *The New Yorker*, and I am glad you do, and that they are there. But *which* were they? I have not heard anything from *The New Yorker* since last autumn, when they sent me a cheque for a not very good piece called 'The Water and the Wine'. That was in late September, I think. Since

> then I have sent them five stories and several poems, and I don't know from Adam which if any they've taken, nor what they have paid me.[8]

When peace eventually came, Sylvia and Valentine were not alone in wondering exactly what kind of new post-war world there was in store for them. Plucky, stoic and at the same time humorously despondent, she explained to a friend:

> No one feels well or happy just now. No one in wartime can quite escape the illusion that when the war ends things will snap back to where they were and that one will be the same age one was when it began, and able to go on from where one left off. But the temple of Janus has two doors, and the door for war and door for peace are equally marked in plain lettering, No Way Back. And the dead are not more irrevocably dead than the living are irrevocably alive. Only yesterday I had an invitation which began, Now that the war is over and things show no sign of getting better I hope you will come and stay. Which puts it into a nutshell well enough.[9]

As in Mollie Panter-Downes' 1940s and '50s stories, the war loomed large in Sylvia's post-war writing, continuing to sketch its impact on the English people, long after the declarations of peace. But slowly change came and life became something else. Her inspired and somewhat unorthodox cooking came into its own after years of rationing. A summer lunch from 1957, for example, consisted of fresh sardines, olives, radish, cucumber with mint and chives and rye biscuit, followed by sweetbreads in cream with green peas (it seems likely that she was one of the many fans of PB 70, Patience Gray's *Plats du Jour* which was the bestselling cookery book of the 1950s).

Sylvia continued writing and her reputation grew larger with her fan-base incorporating new generations of writers including John Updike. Her lauded biography of T H White came out in 1967 and was her greatest success since *Lolly Willowes*. *A Stranger with a Bag*, her last collection of short stories was published in 1966 and 'A Love Match', taken from the collection, won the Katherine Mansfield Menton prize in 1968. And she went on writing stories, including her now cult-ish elfindom ones, well into the 1970s. In total, Sylvia Townsend Warner published eight collections of short stories in her lifetime alongside the seven novels for which she is better remembered. It is her wartime stories, though, that should be on the bookshelf of every Persephone reader in that they perfectly balance the domestic and the political. And they bring such joy with their quick humour and their lively detail.

In January 1968 Sylvia and Valentine celebrated the thirty-seventh anniversary of their 'wedding day'. But Valentine was increasingly unwell with breast cancer. Her death on the morning of 10th November 1969 was the greatest loss of Sylvia's life. 'Her love follows me everywhere,' she wrote and almost immediately began compiling their love letters for publication, busily writing and editing their life together for a general readership. In late 1977 she had a series of falls and by November kept to her bed. She continued to write letters to William Maxwell, spending that bitterly cold winter smoking and reading Wordsworth as the snow fell outside. She died on 1st May 1978. Her final will divided her assets equally between the London Library, the National Trust, the University Federation for Animal Welfare, the National Council for Civil Liberties and the Musicians' Benevolent Fund. The *New York Times* obituary noted her graceful style and ironic wit; what writer could ask for more?

Lydia Fellgett,
London, 2019

1 Sylvia Townsend Warner, Letter to Paul Nordoff, 17:xi:1940 in *Letters* ed. William Maxwell (London: Chatto & Windus, 1982) p67
2 Preface to *Good Evening Mrs Craven* (London: Persephone Books, 1999) pix
3 Letter to Ben Huebsch 29:iii:1941 *Letters* ibid. p71
4 Clare Harman, *Sylvia Townsend Warner: A Biography* (London: Chatto & Windus 1989) p32
5 Letter to Bea Howe, 4:xii:1941 *Letters* ibid. p75
6 Letter to Nancy Cunard 26:vii:1941 *Letters* ibid. p86
7 Letter to William Maxwell 27:x:1962 *Letters* ibid. p204
8 Letter to Paul Nordoff 27:iii:1941 *Letters* ibid. p70
9 Letter to Paul Nordoff 5:ii:1946 *Letters* ibid. p91

ENGLISH CLIMATE:
WARTIME STORIES

THE WATER AND THE WINE

5 October 1940

Because of the fall of the Channel ports, Mrs Hawley at a meeting of the Knitted Comforts for Seamen Circle found herself winding wool off the hands of a stranger, an elderly lady, short, with a jowl, removed from the Isle of Thanet to Hertfordshire. Presently Mrs Hawley found too that the stranger knew the beauties of the neighbourhood better than she did. It turned out that she used to live at Amble.

'Why, *I* live at Amble!' said Mrs Hawley. 'Such a dear little town, so untouched! You wouldn't find it in the least changed. And we have such a charming house – historic, really. Sylvester Gauntlett once lived in it.'

'So did I,' said the lady. 'He was my father.'

'What! Are you Sylvester Gauntlett's daughter? Oh, you must come and have tea and see the house. It's quite simple. The Amble bus –'

'I am old enough to bicycle,' said Miss Gauntlett. 'Let us disregard the bus.'

Mrs Hawley's pleasure was qualified by a sensation that Sylvester Gauntlett's daughter was not worthy of Sylvester

Gauntlett, a writer so polished and whimsical that critics often referred to him as 'that lesser Lamb'. There was nothing whimsical about Miss Gauntlett except her knitting, and that was not polished. But during the course of the weekend Mrs Hawley rearranged the impressions first formed at the meeting of the Knitted Comforts for Seamen Circle, and by the day Miss Gauntlett was due she was expected with the compassion proper towards a dear old lady revisiting the house of her girlhood – 'almost like a ghost,' Mrs Hawley remarked to her daughter.

On arrival, Miss Gauntlett proved less like a ghost than like a verger, a verger implacably resolved on showing tourists round a temporarily obliterated cathedral. Her grip on the past was only equalled by her indifference to the present. She put out any possibilities of a fire on the Hawley's open hearth by the way she said 'Should be a stove', and abolished a whole vista of rambling roses by one glance from a window and the words 'Weren't there.'

Having converted the drawing room to a dining room, she made over the dining room into a parlour. 'A Turkey carpet,' she stated, tramping over the parquet. 'Books here. More books there. A sash window. None of those exposed beams. Green wallpaper – a deep leaf green. Green was my father's favourite colour. And the gas brackets' – the roar of a passing plane overcame her, but when the noise had evaporated, she was ready to go on – 'had very pretty opalescent shades imitating whelk shells. Tiresome, rowdy creatures, one can't get away from them! I might as well have stayed on at Broadstairs.'

'Green,' said Mrs Hawley. 'How interesting! I can't tell you,

Miss Gauntlett, how enthralling it is to be able to picture it all as it was in your father's day. We have so often wondered. Haven't we, Pamela?'

Behind the mother stood the daughter, staring coldly at the chatty old hag whose youth had been illumined by gas, whose father had been yet another of those far too numerous English men of letters.

'Now we shall be able to imagine it all,' Mrs Hawley said. 'The green walls, the books, your father at his desk.'

'My father always wrote in his dressing –'

Another plane flew over. Dressing room, dressing gown? Gown sounded more literary. Mrs Hawley waited with an understanding smile, a smile touched with humour and tender indulgence for the whims of genius, till the plane allowed her to say: 'So much more comfortable!'

'Quieter, at any rate,' Miss Gauntlett allowed. 'Being on the first floor, and at the back.'

A troubled expression crossed Mrs Hawley's countenance. She seemed to be calculating how many floors her house had and, indeed, how many backs.

'I'll show you,' Miss Gauntlett said.

Briskly she walked upstairs and along the landing. Familiarly, as though it were nothing to her to open a door on the shade of a minor master, she opened the door of the bathroom.

'Oh!'

'Did your father write in his bath?' asked the daughter.

'*Darling!*' Mrs Hawley's voice was attuned to a much younger daughter. 'It wasn't a bathroom *then*.'

It was not the recollected figure of Sylvester Gauntlett, stocky and arrogant, with plump hands stained by nicotine and the large head turning with the bull-like regard of its little, twinkling eyes, or the remembered smell of Latakia tobacco that immobilised his daughter on the threshold of Mrs Hawley's bathroom. She saw, as distinctly as if it had actually been there, a tin saucer bath, and beside it a brown hot-water can whose paint, rather scabby with reiterated scaldings, was beginning to peel off; and the smell in her mind's nose was a mingled smell of Old Brown Windsor soap and heated enamel. In the bath, steaming gently, was a shallow lake, perhaps a couple of inches deep. Rising from the lake were legs – the legs of statesmen and warriors and men of letters; the legs of scientists whose opinions cracked the foundations of society and of judges whose verdicts cemented the cracks again; the legs of bishops and the legs of agnostics; aristocratic legs that had been buckled round with the Order of the Garter; and fine, rose-tinted legs that had lain in a royal bed. And among all these were the legs of Sylvester Gauntlett and Sylvester Gauntlett's daughter. Round about the knee all the legs disappeared, lost in the tendrils of steam rising from the two-inch lake.

No one nowadays, thought Miss Gauntlett, has any conception of the comfort, the luxury, the privacy, of a saucer bath in one's dressing room. Turning her eyes from the legs of a past generation to the faces of Mrs and Miss Hawley, she knew that this was exactly the trouble. Such a conception had never occurred to them. They just thought it a rather dirty way of bathing. Not that a bathroom was any novelty to Miss

Gauntlett. The Edith Hotel, Residential, for Ladies, where she had lived for the last twenty years, had two bathrooms on each floor, each bathroom supplied with constant hot water and every convenient accessory, including a tin of cleanser and a mop with which each residing lady was expected to leave the bath as she would wish to find it. No comfort, no luxury, no privacy – and no one a whit cleaner, either. But in Mrs Hawley's silly countenance and in the girl's swimming pop-eyes, Miss Gauntlett read plainly enough their conviction that no amount of saucer baths could remove the dirt of England's golden age.

The crowning unfairness of it all was that no shade of dirt would rest on the memory of Sylvester Gauntlett. Unquestionably clean, he would arise from the saucer bath and shine; and so would they all, the statesmen and the warriors, those who wore the Garter and those whose garters were unloosed at a royal command. But Miss Gauntlett, relict of a bathless order, must inherit all their opprobrium, be badged with all their scum and sullied with all their rinsings, and exist in the eyes of these mere Hawleys as a funny old lady who never took a bath, as a grubby antique.

She pulled herself together. With her small eyes darting furious glances over the white paint and the chromium, she described the dressing room, with its walls of a darker shade of green, its brown paint, its curtains of deep olive-coloured serge. She made it all as dark, as poky, as possible.

Mrs Hawley said that it sounded so cosy.

Downstairs there was tea, white curtains fluttering from open windows, sandwiches that were gone in an instant, the girl fidgeting and eyeing the radio. Presently, Mrs Hawley began to fidget too. She was sorry for the poor revisiting ghost who ate so much, whose false teeth served her badly, who must be feeling so distressed at the changes in her old home, and who would not go. Of course, in the Victorian age visits went on for hours. There was so much leisure then.

'Don't you feel, Miss Gauntlett, that there is much less leisure now than there used to be? One of the things that I feel so specially drawn to in your father's essays is the feeling of leisure. I can't imagine him hurrying over a single sentence.'

'He took more than half an hour to shave.'

'Well, of course, that was a work of time then, wasn't it? No electric razors, no hot water,' Mrs Hawley said. And then she thought: Heavens, I shouldn't have said that! 'What *did* we do before electric kettles?' she asked brightly.

'Used spirit lamps,' replied Miss Gauntlett.

No wonder the poor old thing was upset, Mrs Hawley thought. How awkward it had been about the bathroom – Pamela so tactless, poor child, Miss Gauntlett so angry – though perhaps it was only Gauntlett's daughter resenting the conversion of such a father's dressing room.

'But a garden is always so peaceful, don't you think, so restful? You must let me show you the garden before you go.'

The house was built on a slope, and to reach the garden one had to go downstairs and out through the basement. All the way down the stairs (lemon-coloured distemper, a light matting, clear glass in the place of the old clouded pane darkened by bars and blurred by ivy), Miss Gauntlett was saying to herself: 'Unclean, unclean!'

'Here's one innovation I must show you. We're really quite proud of it, though I'm afraid your father would have thought it almost barbarous.' Mrs Hawley opened a door, switched on a light. It showed a small, windowless room with walls newly painted, furnished with some light chairs, a bridge table, tea things, a first-aid box, a pack of cards. 'Our air raid shelter,' she said.

Miss Gauntlett looked in. As she looked, her face assumed an expression of extraordinary blandness. Her wrinkles smoothed out, her small, angry eyes became clear and serene. 'Ah, yes. The wine cellar.'

Her pointing hand moved from wall to wall. The gesture was no longer that of any mere verger. No, this was the cathedral's bishop himself, graciously displaying the treasures of the episcopal strongroom.

'Claret there. Burgundy below. Champagne there, and brandy. My father never cared for any other kind of spirits. Hock and Moselle. White wines, especially a Hermitage and a Montrachet *aîné*. And there, just by your little red buckets, Imperial Tokay.' With a commanding hand, she switched off the light, closed the treasure house. 'Times have changed, haven't they?' she said.

As Miss Gauntlett bicycled home to her lodgings, she thought how Sylvester Gauntlett, that lesser Lamb, would have capped the situation by some delicate quip about wine being changed into water. But she felt no regret that the epigram was unspoken. She was contented with things as they were.

MY SHIRT IS IN MEXICO

4 January 1941

As soon as the train left London, we went along to the buffet car for a drink. The train was crammed, a wartime train loaded with soldiers and with parties of women and children travelling inland to get away from air raids. It was difficult to move along the corridor; one had to edge one's way past soldiers sitting on their packs, heaps of hand luggage, train-sick children being held out of the window, people queued up sheepishly outside the toilets. But the buffet car was almost empty and looked like something belonging to a different world, with its clean, light-painted walls and red leather upholstery.

We sat down at a little table, and presently the attendant came along with the tariff card. He was a middle-aged man with a good face, innocent and humane like a rabbit's. When I said I'd like a cup of black coffee with rum in it, he made no difficulties, though it was not down on the list.

Coming back with our drinks, he looked at us as though we were already friends of his. The rum was in a measuring glass, and as he poured it into my coffee he said: 'Excuse me mentioning it, madam, but I see from your bag you've been in Mexico.'

His voice was full of confidence and excitement. For a moment I wondered if I shouldn't take a chance on it, but I was feeling tired and unsure of my powers, so I said, honestly: 'No such luck. The bag has, but it's only a loan.'

Now we all looked at the label, which was printed with a gay view of flowers and white-clothed tourists riding on festooned mules. And thinking how hard it must be for a man who apparently wanted to go to Mexico to spend his life travelling in a buffet car from Plymouth to London and back again, I said that the friend who owned the bag had liked Mexico very much.

'Oh, yes, it must be a wonderful country,' he said. 'All those hothouse flowers growing wild, and the volcanoes, and the Mexicans making such wonderful artistic things. And everything so old, and yet, in a manner of speaking, only just beginning. Building roads, and learning to read, and getting vaccinated.'

'Sensible beginnings,' said Valentine.

'Yes, that's right. Oh, I'd like to go to Mexico. It must be beautiful. . . . I've got a shirt in Mexico,' he said.

'How did that happen?' I asked. 'You're one up on me. I haven't got anything in Mexico.'

'It's an uncommon thing to say, isn't it? Oil shares, now, or a cousin – that's to be expected. But not a shirt. It all happened before the war, because of a German gentleman, a refugee. I noticed him the moment he came in – he sat down at that table over there – and I thought to myself: Now, he's somebody. A bald man, and thin as a lath, and most remarkably clean. Bald but not elderly, you understand. Presently he ordered a large coffee and a slice of cake. Well, that didn't tell me much, except a nice manner and a German accent. But when I brought along his order, he'd opened his wallet, and there were his papers spread out – a single to Plymouth and a third-class steamer passage.'

'To Mexico?'

'No, to New York. Well, he didn't say anything I could take hold of. But I'd still got a card up my sleeve – there was the ashtray needed emptying. When I went to change it, he said he didn't smoke. Now, I don't smoke either, so that was a beginning. And once you've got a beginning, it's easy, isn't it? From smoking we got round to seasickness, and then I could ask him if he had crossed the Atlantic. "No," said he, "but now I shall." Living in Plymouth, naturally I know a lot about New York, so I could tell him things he'd find useful. Puddings being called desserts, and luggage baggage, and how you can check it through. He laughed, and said he'd be able to carry all his.'

I could see my way to the shirt now.

'Yes, just a suitcase and what he stood up in. What you'd take away for a weekend – and he was going to America for good and all. But not worried in the least. What's more, he seemed so pleased with what he *had* got. Made me feel his suit to see what good wool it was and told me all about a wonderful pair of silk pyjamas he'd been given. And you could tell from the way he spoke he was the sort of gentleman who knows about clothes – quite a dandy, in fact. He said straight out his shoes were a disappointment to him – they were a gift, too. And he was quite right; they were very poor articles. Then all of a sudden it flashed on me he could have my shirt. It was a very nice shirt. Providential, really – I'd bought it that very morning and was carrying it down with me. I always like to buy my shirts in London. You get a better style. Well, he wasn't the sort of man you can have pretences with, so I told him straight out I'd like him to take my shirt. Wasn't I lucky to have it with me, though?'

'You were,' said Valentine. 'I can't wish anyone better luck than that.'

'Yes, and he accepted it so pleasantly. But what I liked best was the way he opened the parcel and looked at the shirt most carefully – how the buttons were fastened on and all. Examined it all over, he did. If he had just taken the parcel, that wouldn't have been the same thing, would it?'

'And now he's in Mexico?'

'Oh, no. He's in New York. It's the shirt that's in Mexico. With a friend of his. Look, this is the letter he wrote me from New York.'

Often read, always carefully refolded, the thin sheet of paper already had the air of something beginning to be historic:

March 11th 1939.

Dear Friend:

I have to tell you how I have made good journey and am settled here in New York City. And I have meet other friends here also, and I find some work shortly. And the beautiful shirt you gave me, it is not ungratefully that I bestow it to a comrade going to Mexico when he has greater need than I. I do not forget the kindness. I hope you are well and make always new friends. I thank you again.

Cordially,

Renatus Leutner.

PS New York is very fine.

'You must feel happy about that shirt,' I said.

'I do,' he replied. 'It was a blue one, just right for a sunny climate. I've always wanted to go to Mexico.'

FROM ABOVE

18 January 1941

The sharp light of an October morning emphasised the perspective of Albion Terrace, whose small stucco houses with light ironwork steps descending from hooded doorways to pocket handkerchief lawns preserved, so Mr Campion said, better than any other street in London the polite amoral grace of the Regency. Many of the polite amoral Graces of that period had lived and entertained in Albion Terrace; and a campaign to persuade the London County Council to commemorate, with blue and white plaques, the tenancy of some of the better-known light-of-loves, was one of Mr Campion's favourite dinner party gambits.

Now Mrs Campion was standing on her top step, staring vaguely at the sky and shaking a duster without energy. She had pale green eyes, pure as a kitten's, and they looked so much at variance with her small, anxious, sallow face that one had the impression they must have been given her by some rich admirer with more connoisseurship than discretion. She yawned several times, and lowered her gaze. At the bottom of the terrace, just closing the gate of Number 47 behind him, was a policeman; 45 and 43 were empty, and he passed them, but turned in again through the gate of 41 and mounted the steps. And having done with 41 he went on to 39.

'Methodical as the milk,' she observed. At the same moment she realised what his errand must be. But instead of doing any of the things she ought to have done, instead of going indoors to turn off the gas, the electricity, and the water at the mains, instead of packing up the spoons or changing into a street suit she continued to stand in the sun watching the policeman's advance.

Presently she could tell from the fragments of conversation that reached her that her guess was indeed exactly right; but even when her own gate squeaked on its hinges and the policeman had come up the steps and was offering his chest to her steady scrutiny she continued to look attentive and docile and to say nothing.

'Are you the occupier of these premises?'

'I am,' she answered ritualistically. 'That's to say, my husband has just gone off to his office and the charwoman doesn't seem to be coming.'

'A time bomb,' said the policeman, 'has been located in the Mews. In the interests of public safety it is necessary to clear the Terrace. Only temporarily, we hope. Before leaving, which should be done as soon as possible, it would be advisable . . .'

While he spoke she was folding the duster, and smoothing it.

'But what will you do about my husband? He's coming back to lunch.'

'Do not trouble, madam. He will be intercepted.'

Her expression was so queerly unconvinced that he noticed it, and added:

'There'll be notices up, you know, or a barrier. You needn't worry about him.'

And as her expression remained just as unconvinced as before, he resumed his official standing and said:

'Doubtless you could get into communication with him.'

Ready just inside the door were the two suitcases. James had placed them there over a month ago, having packed them himself, a man full of plans and foresight. She ran down to the kitchen to turn off the gas and the electricity and the water at the mains. Then she ran upstairs to change her clothes.

Everything that she passed by reproached her, heaped on her the mute reproaches of the blameless and helpless. She felt as though she were being eyed by countless misjudged and faithful spaniels. *You are leaving us*, blinked chairs and tables and ornaments. *You don't love us any more.*

She stared round the bedroom as she fastened her skirt. She must, she must take something with her, some little portable thing. But what? Obviously, something that James had given her. But again, what? The room was full of things that James had given her, all beautiful, all genuine, and almost all expensive.

She picked up a small white satin pincushion, elaborately puffed and pearled. It was a child-bed pincushion and *Bless the Child and Save the Mother* was picked out on it in small pins, every one of which, James said, was of the period. Once, being in a hurry, she had used two of them. One she had replaced.

The other got lost, and the break in the curly capital *C* was like a tiny almost obliterated scar. She stuffed the pincushion into her handbag.

'O God, O God!' she whispered, running downstairs. Picking up the two suitcases she exclaimed more attentively. They were astonishingly heavy. She found that she could now recall some of the things James had been saying during the afternoon he had packed them: that one might find oneself very inconveniently fixed without a hammer and some good stout nails, that a bottle of whisky weighs very little more than a half bottle, that she would be sorry to lose her malachite box, that Browne's *Pseudodoxia* was a book he had always been meaning to re-read.

She staggered out, and behind her the door closed with a noise like a sighing breath cut short.

Other doors too were opening and shutting, the people of Albion Terrace were in retreat. Here and there from a window left open some bright-coloured curtain waved as though in farewell. Dogs barked and tugged at their leads, an old man went rapidly by in a self-propelling bath chair that was heaped with parcels. Children, pale and walking stiffly, carried little cases, a cat mewed and lurched in a hamper, some canaries sang loudly in a cage.

'How odd! I have neither chick nor child,' thought Dionysia Campion. 'Perhaps that is why I feel so heartless.'

Two women passed her, and as they passed one was saying: 'And when I think that only yesterday I had the chimney-sweep . . .'

The suitcases banged against her legs, and she began to

wonder what one does with suitcases containing all that might remain of one's worldly goods. Refugees, she knew, carried suitcases and were never parted from them. More fortunate people hailed a taxi. But while the taximan was loading on the suitcases it occurred to her that a taxi was only a temporary expedient. She could not drive about in it all day.

'Where to, lady?'

'I'm not quite sure. I've got to think a little. Anyway, drive me somewhere away from here.'

'Quite a lot of people use hotels,' he said. 'Others seem to like railway stations.'

'Just drive, please.'

Sometimes she looked out of the window, sometimes she looked at her watch. Suddenly everything became clear to her. She would leave the suitcases at James's club, he could meet them there for lunch. As for herself, she would take a day off, she would go exploring, she would visit St Paul's.

So much a Londoner that she took London for granted, she had never been inside St Paul's. The taxi driver thought it a very spirited destination, and remarked, as they parted, that plenty of time bombs got nipped in the bud. Stuffing back the child-bed pincushion she agreed cordially. An instant later, standing by the statue of Queen Anne and hearing the whirr of the pigeons' wings overhead, she began to tremble. She mounted a few steps, and then looked upward. The portico seemed to reel towards her, she anticipated the weight of the whole enormous building. A door swung open, she heard sounds of a cough, a voice, a chair scraped along the floor, hammer blows, all melted and enveloped in one vast melodious echo as though these shreds of living were being simmered down in this soup cauldron whose lid was a dome with a cross on it. She turned back, intimidated.

But London was full of things which she had never been taken to see and which it might be amusing to see alone. There was the Soane Museum in Lincoln's Inn Fields. There were all those Wren churches, many of them must still be undamaged, and James could not have taken her to every one of them, for her demeanour in churches was unendearing to any lover of architecture since she always became absorbed in reading about the dead instead of admiring such things as retro-choirs and proportions. There was Greenwich Observatory, where the Astronomer Royal and his telescope still directed themselves to the more permanent phenomena of the heavens. There was the Physic Garden, and Carlyle's House, and Somerset House, and Bedlam.

And immediately in front of her was a telephone booth. In the taxi it had seemed to her that, calmed by a half hour in St Paul's, she would find it less painful to ring up James and tell him he was temporarily evacuated. Tell him she must. It would be heartless to leave him to go back for lunch and learn for himself.

Being so much more assimilable in proportions than St Paul's, the telephone booth seemed cosy and reassuring. Opening her bag she downed the child-bed pincushion and got at the pennies. Perhaps he would be out and she could leave the message with his nice sympathetic secretary.

'Mr Campion? Yes, Mrs Campion (it is Mrs Campion, isn't it?), I'll put you through immediately.'

'Hullo, Dionysia.'

'James.'

'Well? Is anything wrong?'

'James. You'd better lunch at your club.'

'Gas gone off again?'

'No. But there's a time bomb in the Mews, and we're temporarily evacuated. The policeman came just after you'd gone.'

After a pause he said:

'My God!'

After another pause he said in an even more remote and ruminating voice:

'Damn.'

'James. I turned everything off, and I took your suitcase to the club. I left mine there too. I thought perhaps you could have lunch at the club.'

'Oh, all right! But why don't I meet you for lunch? Where are you, by the way?'

'Outside St Paul's. James, I don't think I *can* lunch with you, not while your home is hanging on tenterhooks.'

'That's very sensitive of you. Do you think you could bring yourself to sleep with me tonight?'

'I suppose I ought to see about a room in a hotel?'

'Unless you prefer the Tube, or some dome of many-coloured glass over a Rest Centre.'

No wonder he was cross. What on earth possessed me, she thought, to say *your home*? Isn't it my home too? Our bed, our rosewood dining table, our Adam settee? Deep within her, eating away like the chemical of a time bomb, an invincible ruthfulness responded and said: No! James's home. James's choice, James's taste. James's wife, who was James's home's caretaker.

For now it could not be denied. The policeman had come to her like some draped angel, calling on her to arise and leave the fleshpots of Egypt. At the most, he had promised an absolute departure. At the least he had bestowed a whole day during which her responsibilities to 11 Albion Terrace would be in abeyance, a whole day in which she would be free to gad whither she pleased. How ridiculous of her to think she wanted to see St Paul's. Of course she didn't. That sort of wish was merely a copy-catting of James. Her wishes were bounded by the West End and solitude, were quite simple, base, and ordinary.

What she wished was first to have her hair washed and set, her face massaged, her hands manicured. Then she would like a simple, base, and ordinary lunch, macaroni cheese and lemon pie. Then she would like to go to the gramophone shop and try over a lot of records, sitting in a little cubicle furnished with nothing but an easy chair and an ash-tray. Then she would like a cup of chocolate and a hot muffin. Then . . . Then it would be time to hurry through the falling dusk to see what had happened in Albion Terrace. If it had gone James would break his heart. Poor James! Poor James, anyway. In one minute he had had to learn that his home was balanced on the edge of destruction and that his wife was unfaithful to his home.

With guilty alacrity she jumped on a bus; shameless and nimble as any cat running off with the cold pheasant, she ran off to make the most of her holiday. Hourly becoming more depraved, she told the manicurist all about the time bomb in the Mews, and lapped up the sympathy that followed. At the record shop too she told the man about the time bomb, and he agreed with her that music was what she needed, music was the only possible comfort and solace. She played through an album of songs by Debussy, a type of music that James detested, and went out, having bought nothing, humming to herself a vague incantation of whole-tone scale melodies in her husky voice that was like a pastel, for it smudged and never could stay in tune.

The dusk was falling as the taxi neared Albion Terrace. But it would not be too dark to see the notice at the end of the street. She peered out. There was no notice.

'There was a time bomb here this morning,' said the taxi man, stopping before Number 11. 'But it didn't make it.'

This time the child-bed pincushion made its getaway, and fell in the gutter. Dangling it by its white ribbon loop she mounted the steps and let herself into the dark hallway. Two steps farther, and she fell over the suitcases.

A door opened, a light was switched on.

'Well, Dionysia?'

'Oh dear, I didn't mean to be so late! I meant to be back in time to do the black-out and light a fire for you if we still had a hearth. Then I couldn't. I couldn't face finding it all ruins and smithereens. Was it awful coming back, James, not knowing what to expect?'

'Not at all. I'd rung up the police station.'

Now he looked at the little white bolster she dangled.

'What on earth's that?'

'My pincushion. I just had to take something.'

'Incurable kitsch-cat! What a thing to choose! And did you visit St Paul's with that in your hand?'

'In my bag.'

When he said *St Paul's* she remembered that she had done nothing about booking a hotel bedroom for the night. But as they were now back in Albion Terrace, with any luck that fact would not emerge.

NOAH'S ARK

21 June 1941

'Poor little things,' said Mrs Purefoy. 'I'm afraid they'll find it a bit strange.'

'Nonsense!' replied Mrs Temple briskly. 'They'll be *perfectly* happy. All town children are happier in the country. Think of the Fresh Air Fund. Think of that orphanage that came down for the day from Birmingham. They'll be *quite* happy. It isn't as though their mother were coming too to unsettle them.'

'I'll do my best, I'm sure. Though nothing can take a mother's place.'

'You must send them out of doors, Mrs Purefoy. Send them into the fields (of course you'll explain about shutting gates and not walking over crops or chasing cows or tearing up plants by the roots). Why, it will be a new world to them! They can pick wild flowers and look at the birds and the lambs. I dare say they've never even seen a lamb.'

These were the first evacuated children to be received on the Temple estate. Mrs Purefoy felt that children from a bombed town would arrive, if not in blankets, at least in rags.

She pictured them yellow and thin and bare, like young birds; and, like young birds, with enormous eyes and incessant appetites. But when Malcolm and Venice arrived, their clothes were tidy and their hair was shiny, and they ate so moderately they might almost be gentry children.

Mrs Temple deposited them. And after a few words about happiness and gratitude and pale cheeks she left them.

It was teatime. Scarcely had the first cups been poured out when the children began to talk about air raids. But that, Mrs Temple had said, must not be encouraged. It would make them morbid. So Mrs Purefoy repressed her longing to hear more when Malcolm spoke of how the corpses were heaped up where the old coffee stall used to be, and snatched the cover off the canary, whose songs soon put an end to unsuitable conversation. After tea they were shown round: the bedroom under the thatch, the back-kitchen, the pump, the garden, the privy at the end of the garden, the lane – all mud and celandines – that would take them to school.

The leafless orchard (where later on, Mrs Purefoy explained, there would be apples) was filled with birdsong and carpeted with young nettles.

'Do you eat them?' Venice enquired.

'Eat nettles, my dear?'

'Teacher said people in the country ate nettles. And scraped the burned crusts into the teapot. And boiled dandelion roots. Because they were so poor, Teacher said.'

'Goodness gracious me, no! Why, we eat nice cabbage.'

'Teacher said, Men of England, wherefore plough for the lords who lay ye low?'

'You'll see them ploughing tomorrow, maybe. And the little lambs,' said Mrs Purefoy. Everything was swaying in an urgent spring wind and both children looked cold, so they went indoors.

Because of an epidemic of measles the school was closed. On the next morning Mrs Purefoy sent the children out for a walk, giving them careful directions about gates and arable and not having anything to do with the little Dominys. Gravely they set out, gravely they returned, and offered their bunch of primroses to their hostess politely.

The primroses were tied up with an old bootlace which they had found in a hedge.

'And did you see the little lambs?'

'Yes, Mrs Purefoy. We saw quite a lot of lambs.'

'And didn't you think the lambs very pretty?'

'Very pretty. But they aren't white, not all of them. Some of them were grey and spotty-looking.'

'Yes, dears. That's the kind of lambs they are.'

'Oh! Well, they were very nice all the same. Have you ever seen a tiger?'

'No, I can't say that I have.'

'We know several tigers. Especially a tigress called Queenie. She's nine years old, and when she licks you can hear her tongue. She's very sweet-tempered really, and underneath she's a lovely lemon-colour. But when she gets in a temper you should just see her. She yowls and shakes the bars of her cage, and her hair stands out, and as for her claws . . .'

'What dread hands,' murmured Venice. 'And what dread feet?'

‘Yes, my dear, their claws must be dreadful. Let alone their teeth.’

‘And when she thinks her dinner’s coming she goes weaving round like a dance, and purrs.’

‘But the polar bear,’ Venice broke in, ‘is much more dangerous, though he looks kind. His little head comes up out of the water, and he looks round with his little teeny-weeny eyes. And if you were on the rock he’d give you one biff with his paw. And you’d be dead. But most likely he wouldn’t trouble to eat you. He’d just roll you over with his paw, and snuff at you.’

‘*I* think he’d eat her,’ said Malcolm; and frowned at his sister for her lack of courtesy. Unheeding, Venice went on to tell Mrs Purefoy about panthers, jaguars, and a fight she had seen between two crocodiles. She described the scene so vividly that Mrs Purefoy dreamed of crocodiles all night.

The next day it rained heavily. Mrs Temple had not indicated what course should be followed with children when they can’t be sent out of doors, but Mrs Purefoy, with a feeling she had hit on the right thing, went off to a neighbour and borrowed a Noah’s Ark. It was only a qualified success; after a little while they went back to the horsehair sofa and sat talking in low voices. Presently, to Mrs Purefoy peeling potatoes, it emerged that they were discussing someone called Flora, who was dear to them.

‘Who’s Flora, my pretty? A relation of yours?’

‘No. At least, she wasn’t. But she’s dead.’

‘Deary me, how sad! And do you miss her a great deal?’

‘Oh, yes! No end. Oh, she was so lovely! She had big blue eyes, and because her mother died Mr Butcher brought her up himself with a bottle. And she knew us quite well, she really did recognise us.'

'What a sweet little thing! What did she die of, then?' *There, I shouldn't have asked that,* she said to herself. *It doesn't do to ask about deaths, nowadays.*

'Some fool gave her a kipper, Mr Butcher said. Poor darling Flora! Now there's only Jimmy, he's handsome, but terribly wild. Have you ever seen a caracal, Mrs Purefoy? It's like a very big cat, but it has tassels on its ears. As big as a dog. Bigger than most dogs. Flora was a gentle one, but mostly you can't go near them.'

They were back on their wild animals again.

That night Mrs Purefoy was chased by baboons, and found herself trying to feed an anteater from a hot-water bottle.

Mr Purefoy, however, enjoyed the wild animals a great deal. As he was the shepherd, this showed magnanimity. He might have been expected to resent the implied slur on the charms of his lambs. Actually, being a shepherd, Mr Purefoy had exhausted those charms, and found lions a pleasant change. He bought the children a drawing book and some coloured chalks, and commissioned works of art, such as Tigers pulling down an Elephant, or A Boa Constrictor climbing a palm tree after a Bear; and when neighbours dropped in he would display the pictures and call on the artists to tell more.

They complied most willingly. Questioned on any other subject, they retreated into a cautious melancholy reserve, but once launched upon their circle of friends in their hometown zoo they talked with passionate animation, and with the superb social calm of those who describe dukes and duchesses in their native habitats. And for hours after they would look pink and proud, and at ease in their new surroundings. As Mrs Purefoy said, regretfully admitting what she could not approve and could not deny, it was as though wild beasts were meat and drink, home and mother, to those poor dear children.

The red and yellow chalks gave out first; then came a spell of bears, camels, and walruses; crocodiles and trees exhausted the green chalk, and the blue was expended on baboons, the heavens, and a few rather grudging birds. When only the purple chalk was left Mr Purefoy sought to commission a rhinoceros. The children shook their heads. They had no purple friends.

'But here be a green monkey?'

'He was green,' explained Malcolm.

'Not quite *so* green. But a greeny colour.' added Venice.

Mr Purefoy said:

'Well, think of that!'

For Mr Purefoy was able to think with calm pleasure of green monkeys. Mrs Purefoy was not so happily constituted, even a modest brown or grey monkey, entirely unrelieved by brighter tints, was enough to get into her dreams and worry her; and a word used by Mrs Temple returned to her thoughts, and strengthened her in a conviction that it would do the children no good to be always talking of their menagerie. *Morbid.* That was the word. Surely it was morbid to be for ever dwelling on tigers and serpents, and evoking frightful unsurmised aspects of creation called Binturongs, and Peccaries, and Kinkajous. It was as morbid as talking about corpses heaped up where the old coffee stall used to be; and having denied herself the corpses which she would have taken a natural pleasure in, it seemed hard to Mrs Purefoy that she must endure tigers and kinkajous.

So presently she was able to convince herself in good faith that it was very sad for the poor children to have so many wild animals imprinted on their memories; that just as other evacuated children one heard of had lice in their heads, the heads of Malcolm and Venice were infested with carnivores. It was no fault of theirs, poor little things, just a token of what town children are exposed to; and with all the zeal of self-delusion she endeavoured to distract them from their painful recollections and secret fears. Since the local fauna interested them only as remembrancers of wild beasts, she thought they might be weaned away into the vegetable kingdom, and gave them each a small plot in the garden, and a trowel, and some packets of radish and turnip seed. They dug; and dug up worms; and the worms recalled snakes, and in a moment the garden was, so Mrs Purefoy felt, crepitating with cobras and rattlesnakes.

But the crisis of Mrs Purefoy's compassion was not reached till the afternoon when Venice began talking about wolves.

It was the worse for beginning with a misunderstanding – Venice's account of playing with wolf cubs being taken by her hostess as referring to play with members of the Junior Branch of the Boy Scouts. Mrs Temple approved of the Scout movement. It was the antithesis of being morbid. And Mrs Purefoy, feeling that here at last might be the answer to prayer, said encouragingly:

'You know, there are several cubs here.'

'Oh! Are there? Where are they? When can I see them?'

'Whenever you like, I dare say. Perhaps they could come to tea.'

'Malcolm! Did you hear? Mrs Purefoy says there are some wolf cubs here, and that we could have them to tea. How I'd love to play with wolf cubs again, and rub my nose in them, and snuff up their funny smell!'

'Why not be a Brownie?' said Mrs Purefoy discriminatingly. 'That's for little girls, you know.'

'But what could we feed them on, Mrs Purefoy? They don't really like anything but meat. And meat's rationed. Perhaps you could get them some *old* meat. Or some horseflesh.'

'Venice, dear!'

'Who keeps their mother, Mrs Purefoy? Is she a big one?'

'*Malcolm*! Don't be rude! I can't ask any little boys to tea if you are going to talk like that.'

Malcolm turned pale, and began to expostulate. But his words were obliterated by Venice, who was swinging round and round with her eyes shut, and chanting:

When the wolf that nightly prowls
Bays the moon with hideous howls.
Wa-oo! Wa-oo! Hideous howls!

'Hush, child, for heaven's sake. Whatever's come over you?'

'Venice loves wolves,' her brother explained.

'Hideous howls! We're going to play with wolves. We're going to smell of wolf. Not even with scented soap you can't wash the smell off. Oh, Mrs Purefoy, why didn't you tell us before there are wolves here?'

Shuddering, Mrs Purefoy said:

'I never told you any such thing. I was talking about nice little children, not savage beasts.'

Venice stopped in her dance. Her hair, still whirling, swept across her eyes. Malcolm put his arm around her.

'Oh well, it can't be helped. Come on, Venice. You couldn't really expect wolves in the country, you know.'

But Mrs Purefoy had never felt quite so sure. Lions, tigers, rattlesnakes, they belonged to foreign parts. Wolves were nearer the bone. There had been wolves in England, and might be again. The neighbourhood of a shepherd's cottage was just where they might be expected, and if anything would fetch them that child's bloodcurdling screeches would. She sat down heavily, and began to tremble, and was still trembling when her husband came in.

'If this dwelling on wild animals goes on, George, I shall have to say something to Mrs Temple.'

Only desperation, he realised, could speak thus. For himself, he would have preferred any amount of wild animals, dwelled on or dwelled with, to an intervention by the lady of the manor. He set himself to reason with his wife, at first admitting artfully that all this menagering would get on anyone's nerves, but developing the great truth that if it isn't one thing it's another, and that if Malcolm and Venice were not so set on their fancy animals they might turn to real ones, trying to milk cows, falling into pigsties, or bringing home – he had heard of such things – snakes, lizards, and hedgehogs.

Then he worked on her softer nature, and finally on her chivalry, declaring it was bad enough for children to to be bombed without having Mrs Temple after them into the bargain. And when Mrs Purefoy had passed from interruptions to sobs, and from sobs to smoothing her apron, he judged it safe to conclude:

'What's more, I won't have it. You leave them be!'

Upstairs Malcolm was saying:

'After all, it wouldn't be much good even if there were wolves here. They'd milk them, or kill them like their own silly animals.'

No wife gives way unreservedly. Mrs Purefoy now took to sighing at the names of outlandish animals as though such names were blasphemies. But Mr Purefoy bought another set of coloured chalks, and commissioned more scenes of natural history, expressing a particular passion for ocelots, gnus, Tasmanian Devils, and pandas; and Mrs Purefoy relapsed into her earlier stronghold: that it was dreadful for the poor little things to be so obsessed by all those awful creatures they had been driven to take up with because town life has no natural pleasures for children, and that she only prayed it wouldn't come out in their dreams. Indeed, at the last it was with an almost genuine benevolence that she handed a copy of the paper across the table.

'Here's something you'll be interested in, my dears.'

Beside a small paragraph her thumbnail had made a deep indentation. *Owing to the continuance of blitz bombing the authorities of the Plymouth Zoo have caused all the dangerous animals to be destroyed.*

The girl stared in front of her and the boy, with desperate solicitude, stared at the girl. *O God,* he prayed, *O God, don't let her cry*! She did not cry.

Their Ark, so brightly painted, so gloriously companied, had foundered under them. They swam on the waste of waters, and for a little it seemed that a few small harmless beasts swam with them; but presently these disappeared, and nothing broke the surface except a distant unpeopled Ararat. As Mrs Purefoy remarked, you could see with one eye what a weight had been lifted off their minds. By the time the school re-opened they were drawing bombers and stoning water rats like any other children about the place.

SETTERAGIC ON

13 September 1941

Mr Purvey (Thomas A Purvey, Tobacconist) laid down his penknife and held out a square of pasteboard at arm's length. At the same time, to get the maximum vista, he leaned his head back and half-closed his eyes.

'Pretty good. Pret-ty good. Not *quite* perfect, though.'

He was a small man, and weedy. His hair was thinning on top, his ears were pale and unarticulated and suggested mushrooms. From head to foot he seemed to have been contrived thriftily, nourished sparingly. There was nothing abundant about him except his eyelashes, which were thick and even, like a doll's.

He gave the penknife a deft stroke or two over the carborundum, and went on picking at the lettered pasteboard.

'There, Doreen! How will that do?'

'Looks all right.'

'Another advantage of doing it in stencil,' he said, apparently continuing some private conversation, for to his wife he had not mentioned any previous advantages, 'it will do just as well when the black-outs come round again. Six o'clock on a

November evening, lights on in here, dark outside. They'll be able to read it without coming in. No draughts, you see. No wet umbrellas dripping all over the place. That is, of course, if it is still needed then.'

'If *it* is, we shan't be,' she said.

The words were like bubbles rising through stagnant water. They seemed to have no relevance to the woman who uttered them, a woman who sat behind the counter and knitted, her head with its elaborate top knot bent over her work, her lips continuously stirred as she registered stitch after stitch.

When he had fixed the pasteboard on the glass panel of the door he went out and examined it from the street. Returning, he went into the back of the little shop and began to tidy some drawers. Only then did she raise her eyelids and look at the stencilled pasteboard. Presently her lips began to stir again, but this time to a different rhythm.

SETTERAGIC ON. OCCABOT ON.

Other words in that crow's language were TAM HTAB, GNIKOMS, and MOOR TELIOT. Crow's language, crow's lettering too, with the letters turned backwards, as children write them, chalking on blank walls words they ought not to know. Through the stencilled crannies she could catch minute bright aspects of the world outside; and thus beheld, the sea seemed bluer, and the billows of barbed wire more sharply jagged and intricate than when seen through the rest of the glass door-panel, or between the pyramids of dummy packets in the shop window.

Staring at these prismatic aspects of the July afternoon she found herself hearing the wind.

At first she hardly knew that it was the wind. There was nothing in the view, the blue sea and cloudless sky, the few passers-by strolling hatless and in summer clothes, to suggest a wind blowing. The noise seemed more like something mechanical, unrelated to weather. It was more like the noise of a bomber than the noise of the wind.

Then, with no cadence, no diminution, it left off – left off as though it had been turned off. If it had been a bomber, she thought, I would have been under the counter by now. But actually the houses along the seafront were the safest houses in the town, for the bombers waited to have their target well under them before they let go.

The noise returned, pulsing and strident, and rose to the former pitch, and continued for a while, and again seemed to be turned off.

'Tom! Do you hear that? That's the wind.'

'Getting up, isn't it? I say, Doreen, we've got another gross of pipe-cleaners. What a pity we didn't know it when everybody was asking for them, and they were so short. And seven more of those Jubilee cigar cases.'

'Bit late, isn't it?'

'No, why? I'm going to put them out, anyway. After all, they're patriotic, that brings them up to date. Historic, too.'

'Pity you can't find a fag, Tom. That would be historic, all right.'

He came out with a trayful of his oddments, and began rearranging the glass showcase. She moved to one side and stood watching him.

'Tom. Tom, what shall we do?'

'What do you mean, dear?'

'You know what I mean, all right. What shall we do if this shortage goes on? We can't live by selling extras, even if people are fools enough to buy them.'

''S'only temp'ry,' he said; and pulling out a silver lighter he began to polish it on his sleeve.

'Temporary? And what did we hear six months ago? Do you remember that evacuee woman from Sheffield, who said you couldn't get any up in the north for love or money? And what about all the tommies, that lot from the Midlands, who used to buy fags to send home? That was soon after Christmas, that was. And what about those letters in the papers, round about Easter, saying that women ought not to be allowed to smoke? Temporary? So's creeping paralysis.'

His elbow knocked a display card. It fell with a clatter, and brought down a structure of dummy cartons with it. But listening to the wind she did not seem to hear.

'But you heard what it said on the wireless. There's never been so much tobacco let out as there is now. After all, you can't go against facts, Doreen.'

A woman, passing, stopped and looked searchingly in the window. She came in.

'Good afternoon. I want some cigarettes. I expect anything you have got will suit me, I'm really not a bit particular about the brand.' She spoke jauntily, airily, and flipped a ten-shilling note on the counter.

'I'm sorry, madam. But we have no cigarettes.'

'Goodness! Getting quite rarities, aren't they? Well, I don't mind rolling my own for a change. One must be adaptable, mustn't one, in wartime? What tobacco have you got?'

'We have no tobacco either, madam.'

'No tobacco? Worse and worse! Well, I suppose you've got pipe tobacco, some sort of shag. I'm not particular. Or cigars, those little cigars?'

'No pipe tobacco either, madam. Nor cigars. No tobacco whatsoever.'

Shrugging her shoulders she turned to go. Pausing, she turned back an altered face, and said humbly:

'I want it for my husband, you know.'

After she had gone Doreen exclaimed: 'Fool! Hasn't she got eyes in her head? *I* can read that board backside forward. Setteragic on! Occabot on!'

'What, dear?'

She pointed to the board on the door.

'So it does,' he said with interest. '*Setteragic on*. Sounds funny, doesn't it?'

'Funny as the wind,' she said. 'What does it mean, howling its head off on a boiling hot day in midsummer, and not a cloud in the sky? Lunatic, I call it.'

'It's past midsummer, though. The longest day was nearly three weeks ago.'

'That's right! Now you tell me the days are beginning to draw in.'

'I expect it means a change in the weather,' he said. 'It often does, a wind at this time of year. I do miss the weather forecasts on the wireless, I must say. Though of course we couldn't have spies reporting them to the enemy. I think I shall make one of those seaweed barometers. They're very good, I believe, very reliable. They get moist when it's going to rain.'

All of a sudden she bowed her head, pressing her cheek to the glass top of the showcase.

'Oh God, Tom! I shall go mad if I can't get a smoke.'

A shadow darkened the doorway, paused, and went on.

'It's a pity I'm such a fool, isn't it? But it's this silly wind, howling for no earthly reason, that gets me down. And the smell in this shop, and all the dummies grinning at me all round. And then what you said about the days drawing in, and the black-outs and the air raids beginning again.'

He put his arm round her waist, his glance meanwhile straying about the shop. 'If we could sell the business . . .'

'If a bomb would fall on the business!'

'If we could sell the business, maybe we could move somewhere quieter. Plenty of jobs I could get now, you know, even with my feet. Maybe before the winter . . .'

'More likely I'll be called up by then. Well, they say making munitions takes your mind off it. Here's another fool that can't read.'

This time the customer opened the door; but he had walked on again while the doorbell still jangled. Thomas shut the door and went to the back of the shop.

'Tom,' she said, after a while, 'I've been thinking. Isn't it funny? – if we were out in this wind, you know, we should say how refreshing it was. Blowing the cobwebs away, and all that.'

'Talk of cobwebs, you ought to see this cupboard. It must be a year since I gave it a proper turnout. More. Here's one of those Munich mascots that were among the stock we took over.'

'And if it were raining,' she continued, 'properly stormy, and one could see the clouds moving and the breakers out at sea, that would be all right, too. Sort of cosy and adventurous. But to sit here on a glaring fine afternoon listening to a wind that's doing nothing – I'd rather it blew the roof off. Tom! Do you suppose that what I'm really pining for is another go of air raids?'

'I'm sure it's the very last thing.'

His tone was kind and reassuring, and only slightly inattentive. And because his head was buried in the cupboard he sounded as though he were speaking from some religious compartment, a pulpit or a confessional. She looked at his dusty back, where a scrap of cellophane was poised like a butterfly.

Fossicking in that cupboard, she thought. Always busy, always inventing something to be busy about. Always about nothing. Make-believe. It's a spade and bucket he should have really.

She smiled, pinching in the corners of her mouth and nodding to herself. A spade and bucket was just what he had got, and some nice sand into the bargain. She looked at the ARP outfit, neatly grouped in the corner. Another poor fool had paused to contemplate the lying window.

'Strain,' continued the voice in the cupboard. 'Just strain. And one way or another way, we all feel . . . Good Lord! Doreen! *Doreen!* I've found a box of fifty!'

He hurried forward, shaking, but still remembering to blow the dust off the lid. She turned as though set on fire. And the doorbell jangled, and a second convulsion turned them, quietly attentive, towards the customer.

'Good afternoon,' he said. He smiled, and his voice was cordial. 'It's all right, I'm not after fags. I believe what you say on the door, though I wouldn't in most establishments. But being back in the old place I thought I'd just look in, and ask how you're getting along.'

He was a tall fellow, and one could see that even a little while before he had been dashingly handsome, with a swarthy satanic beauty; but now he looked a shabby Satan, at once aggressive and devitalised. And not even an expensive new suit could mask the sagging lines of his shoulders, the heaviness of physical strength going stale.

'You don't remember me, I gather.'

'Yes, I do,' she said. 'You're Mr Martin, you used to be at the Esplanade Garage.'

'That's me. Nothing wrong with your memory, Mrs Purvey.'

He turned his dark gaze on her, a glittering broadside; but the effect was marred by a nervous twitch that closed up one eye.

'And now you're doing aircraft production, aren't you? What's it like, up there?'

'Well, some says one thing, and some says another. Yes, it's a Valley of the Shadow factory all right. But I don't mind it. Still, it's nice to be out for a bit.'

'On a holiday?' asked Mr Purvey.

'Well, I'm here and not there.'

'What? You mean to say you just marched out? Will they take you back?'

He looked at his right hand, scarred and sinewy, with its short nails newly polished.

'They'll take me back all right, Mrs Purvey. They aren't so straitlaced as some, they'll take me back.'

'Absenteeism, eh?' said the tobacconist. 'What they write about in the newspapers. Mind you, I can see your side of it too. A seven-day week and overtime. The human frame can't really stand it.'

'But the money's good,' she said.

'Money's all right. But what's the sense of having money when there's nothing to buy with it? What's the sense of it? All my life I've wanted to smoke cigars, and couldn't afford them. Now I can afford them with as much gold bandaging as an Admiral. And I can't get them.'

'Still, it's our duty to save,' said Mr Purvey.

His face twitching, the young man looked round the shop. With every contraction the left side of his upper lip was pulled up as though he were about to snarl. The husband and wife exchanged glances, and Mr Purvey pushed the box of fifty a little farther under cover.

After a long survey of the wares the young man bought a silver-hooped tobacco jar.

'Do to keep my ends in,' he said. 'When I've got ends.'

The wind, steadily rising to the same pitch, hung for a while on its shrill note and was shut off.

'Quite a storm getting up,' she said.

‘I should say so. I was passing the scenic railway on my way here, and saw it rip off a bit of canvas, the bit painted like rocks and a waterfall, easy as cutting butter. Poor old scenic! Nobody goes there now, I suppose?’

‘No. It’s been closed for a long while. No more holiday people now, you see. Not allowed.’

‘I used to enjoy the scenic,’ he said. ‘Like a kid, I did. It used to feel quite dangerous, too, didn’t it, round the bends? I remember one day I was on the scenic, and a pansy in the seat in front of me he got so upset he fell on his knees and began to pray. Shut his eyes and prayed about the hour of his death to everything in heaven.’

For a moment his laugh was genuine; but as they echoed it it became false as theirs.

‘Roman Catholic, I suppose,’ said Mr Purvey.

‘Times are changed, aren’t they? There was a lot of fun in those days, though. Everything was pretty pleasant. Fish and chips, and no particular hurry, and half-days regular, and the esplanade all lit up at night, and the band playing, and a fag whenever you wanted it. Well, half the time you don’t know when you’re lucky.’

Her hand moved towards the box. Mr Purvey shoved it a little farther away.

‘Here for long?’ he asked.

‘Going back tomorrow like a good boy. Not taking any smokes with me either, though I hoped I would. I thought you’d still got them down here.’

‘They don’t come in as they did,’ said the tobacconist. ‘And they go in a flash. Everyone’s after them. I can’t make it out.

They said on the wireless there's never been so much tobacco let out as there is now.'

'Somebody's getting them!' she exclaimed. 'Stands to reason somebody's getting more than their fair share. What I'd like to know is, who?'

'Well, it isn't me, Mrs Purvey, I know that. And it isn't you either, judging by that card in your door. I did see one packet of twenty up the town, but they wouldn't let me have it because I wasn't a regular customer.'

'One has to do it that way,' said Mr Purvey, standing his ground between his wife and the shelf towards which her hand sketched a wavering movement.

'Hard on you folk too, I reckon.'

'We must hope for better times,' said Mr Purvey. 'And it's the people in your job who are bringing those better times nearer. Better times for all concerned. So you're going back tomorrow? Well, I'm sure we both wish you the best of luck.'

'Stop and have a cup of tea. Do, Mr Martin! I always make a cup about this time.'

Her voice, at once urgent and hesitating, seemed to charge the words with a dare. He stared at her, blinking, as though she were a light suddenly turned on. Her face assumed an expression of desperation, of terror.

'Tom! Just go and put the kettle on the gas ring.'

Tom did not move.

'It's very kind of you, Mrs Purvey. But I think I'd better be getting along, all the same. So here's Cheerio and Goodbye!'

When the door had shut, when the bell had rocked itself to silence, they turned and looked at each other.

'Oh God, aren't we awful? Why did you stop me?'

'Good thing if I did. You need them as much as he does. More. You know how you feel if you can't get your smoke, Doreen.'

'You know what my temper's like if I don't, more like it.'

He pulled out his handkerchief and began to wipe the tears off her cheeks. Having last been used in the cupboard the handkerchief was dusty. She sneezed.

'Oh Tom, you're worse than a mother, really you are.'

'And it's my duty to look out for you,' he continued. 'That's how I look at it. You first, the rest nowhere. And if it was waggonloads of Martins, you'd come first. It's natural. Now why don't you have one now, slip away into the back, and have one?'

She opened the box, drew a deep breath, ran her finger delicately along the ribbed ranks under the paper bind.

'No. I'll wait till this evening, till I can give my whole mind to it. You must smoke some too, Tom. We must share and share alike.'

'Well, just one to keep you company,' he said.

RAINBOW VILLA

18 October 1941

'So I have decided to come back.'

Her face was flushed, for she had spoken at length, and with vehemence. Now, realising that it was not usual to pour out such confidences, and so energetically, to the house agent, she added with sharper decision and a grander manner:

'Quite decided. I am positive it is what my dear brother would have wished. And I have ordered the furniture to come from the repository next week.'

At the mention of the dead the house agent's face took on an easier posture. The expression with which one acknowledges a dead client is formalised, familiar, calling for no difficult adjustments.

'Ah! One does not see many people like Mr Ensor nowadays.'

'I dare say not.'

The flush had died away, leaving her face pale with the dirty pallor of age. The vehemence had died away too. She was thinking that Francis would not have approved this promiscuous washing of family dirty linen. There had been no need to tell Mr Genge that living with Florence had turned out badly, and certainly no need to describe how silly Florence had been about bacon and air raids. It should have been sufficient to say that she had decided to come back to Rainbow Villa, where she had lived for so long with Francis, where now she would live alone. On the desk between them a ledger lay open. The house-agent looked again at the clean page, so elegantly written, so singularly free from erasures and additions that it resembled a tombstone.

But he looked at it as though it were so importantly full as to be almost undecipherable.

'November 1938. Nine-teen-thir-ty-eight. Practically three years ago.'

'Two years and eight months.'

'The war,' said Mr Genge. 'The war. It seems to emphasise the lapse of time, does it not?'

'Do you find it so? I can't say that I notice much difference. Time seems to go about as fast as usual. Of course, I can remember several wars,' said the old lady.

'Seeing so many changes,' said the house agent, 'being, so to speak, on the spot, and seeing them personally, makes pre-war days seem quite distant days. War brings changes. That is inevitable. We must bow to it.'

He looked so bowed, all of a sudden, that Miss Ensor said:

'I hope you have not had any bereavements.'

'No. No, not actually. Actually not. But one sees so many changes. Especially, perhaps, in my profession. Changes of ownership. Changes of tenancy. Changes . . .'

His tone indicated that the changes were mostly for the worse.

‘No doubt,’ said she. ‘However, I don’t expect to find Rainbow Villa much changed. It is really providential that you couldn’t find me a tenant for it.’

No failure on his part, but the exorbitant rent she insisted on demanding for that small and unattractive house was the reason. But the representative of Messrs Angel, Genge and Chilmaid replied, sadly and meekly:

‘No, we failed over the tenant. But of course one must bear in mind that the house has not been wholly unoccupied.’

‘Oh, that billeting business. Poor fellows, I was very glad to think of them there, with a sound roof over their heads.’

Mr Genge gazed into his book.

‘December thirty-nine to March forty. Twelve weeks. Thirty-five men.’

‘Shocking!’ said Miss Ensor. ‘Such overcrowding. But better than tents.’

‘Oh, undoubtedly. The only possible, the only patriotic view to take. Better than tents. Yes. Particularly as the season was so severe. Yes, indeed! Which reminds me, I fear you may find a few little dilapidations. A little damage to the interior woodwork. Some of the palings missing.’

‘Why?’

‘The weather, you know. Such unusually low temperatures. In fact, I think they may have helped themselves to a little firewood. Very natural. A way they have in the army you know.’

‘H’m.’

‘Of course,’ Mr Genge continued, ‘we submitted our claim to the War Office. The forms went through some time ago. To the appropriate department.’

'Well, haven't they paid yet?'

'I think not. No. Actually, not quite yet. But, of course they will. It is merely a question of a little patience.'

'They should have done it long ago,' she said. 'What else was damaged?'

'Oh, very little, considering. A pane or two of glass. Various small fixtures. I think the schedule is downstairs. I could have it brought up to you if you wish.'

His hand hovered over the desk telephone.

'Don't trouble. I can see for myself, for I'm going there now. I am catching the midday bus.'

'No, no!' exclaimed Mr Genge. 'That we cannot permit. Our junior partner, Mr Brown, will drive you in his car.'

His tone of voice had become suddenly warm, free, bestowing.

'Oh, very well. That will be very kind of him.'

There was no answering warmth and reception. With the flippancy of old age she seemed to regard Mr Brown and the bus as pretty well equivalent. And while Mr Genge was implying down his telephone that Miss Ensor was the most precious, the most highly valued, of all the firm's clients – as Mr Brown would, of course, be aware – she was unconcernedly reading the notices of fat stock and farm implements for sale by auction.

To Mr Brown, who had not seen her before, Miss Ensor seemed unbelievably old: so old that if she had fallen to pieces under the strong midday sun of July, beating down on the street, it would have been a quite natural confirmation of words he had heard once or twice from Mr Genge on the subject of Rainbow Villa . . . *She'll* never need the house again!

But instead of falling to pieces Miss Ensor climbed into the car as nimbly as a spider.

A jolt, he thought, might finish her yet. But though his agitated misery made him drive abominably, jolts did nothing to Miss Ensor beyond swinging her hat a little farther over one eye.

For Mr Brown was a compassionate young man, and so much disliked the thought of any unpleasantness, any sight of suffering, that he had prepared himself to be a conscientious objector, not knowing that the state of his aorta would reserve him for civilian sufferings only. Miss Ensor however turned to him briskly and said:

'Why aren't you in the army, young man?'

'My heart,' murmured Mr Brown; and thinking that she was probably a rather nasty old lady, rude and overbearing, became even more afflicted: for it is doubly painful to be sorry for people you can't like.

'H'm.'

They drove in silence for some miles. He thought of mentioning the country, the prospects of a good harvest, the changes . . . no, no, good God! Not changes! Not with that wrecked building awaiting them, the mammocked billet of thirty-five freezing soldiers, that Aunt Sally of evacuee children, that doss-house of tramps, that habitation of stray cats and foxes. Suppose that at the moment they arrived a tramp . . .?

Before he knew what the words would be he had asked:

‘Why Rainbow? Why was it called Rainbow Villa?’

‘My brother named it.’

They took the right-hand fork. The road swung between fat hedges, everything in sight looked arrogantly green, arrogantly thriving. If only the house had creepers on it, ivy, ampelopsis, anything to muffle the first impact, make the truth less raw . . .! But it hadn’t. And again his thoughts returned to the question, Why Rainbow? – of all names the silliest for a bare square box of drab roughcast, standing like a sentry box at the side of the road staring at the landscape with blank rectangular eyes, three above and two below.

‘I’m afraid it may be rather a shock . . .’

But the words had been got out too late, for already the car had rounded the bend and the shock had been received. He drew up. After a minute she began to scrabble at the window-lever, saying:

‘How does this thing work? I want to get out.’

In his hand the keys of the house flashed. At Angel, Genge and Chilmaid all keys were polished regularly, such small details make a good impression. But there was no need of them, for the door was off its hinges. Instead, he lifted aside the porch of flimsy wire trellis, which had collapsed across the threshold.

A stab of light fell on the sitting room floor, coming through the hole in the roof and the great gap in the flooring of the room above. It shone on a piece of crumpled paper, on which was printed: *To Let. Apply Messrs Angel, Genge and Chilmaid, House Agents, Estate Agents and Auctioneers, Market-place, Durnford.* It shone, too, on splinters of broken glass and on excrements. They crossed the passage to the corresponding room. Here, too, was broken glass; but it had been swept into a corner, and the centre of the room was occupied by a bed of withering bracken fronds. On the hearth were some toe-rags, and the scattered ashes of a fire, and a rusty kettle and two beer bottles stood nearby.

Looking upward, Mr Brown said in a voice of dreamy misery:

'The ceiling of this one seems pretty sound.'

Silent, she walked out. He followed her to the foot of the stairs. Steps and banisters had been hacked away.

'I don't know if it's worth while going up. I will, if you like.'

Still silent, she turned and went into the kitchen, and on from there to the scullery. There was a scuffling noise, and a cat leaped out of the copper.

'Poor thing! Poor pussy!'

Her voice reminded him of a doll his sister had had, a doll which when you pulled its strings said: *Papa! Mamma!*

Standing behind her, ravaged with embarrassment and incompetent pity, he actually began to wring his hands. After a while she moved over to the copper, and looked inside.

'No kittens.'

Had she gone mad, an octogenarian Ophelia, or was she revenging herself by playing on his feelings? When he heard a car approach and halt outside, he was so desperate that he really believed that Mr Genge, repenting, had followed in order to take on himself the burden of this ghastly situation. But the car door did not open; and presently two voices, ladylikely loud, were heard.

'Isn't it frightful? A direct hit. We've had quite a lot of them round here, you know.'

'Looks more like blast to me.'

'Oh, do you think so? I wonder where the crater is. Did I tell you about Penelope's landmine? Of all the amazing strokes of luck . . .!'

Fortunately the old lady was rather deaf. But the visiting voices were loud, and their diction was clear, and agonised by the thought that Miss Ensor might at any moment hear her property (suffering, so Mr Genge said, from the inevitable dilapidations of a house left empty in wartime) mistaken for a bombed house, Mr Brown raised his own voice.

'It's chiefly the woodwork, you know. It was so fearfully cold that winter, and some little delay, I understand, about coal. We have sent in a claim for that and for the windows. Though to do the men justice, some of the windows have gone since. There are so many children about now . . . rather wild children. I often wonder if it's seeing all the wreckage in blitzed towns that makes them so destructive when they are sent down here. Psychological, you know. Of course, the roof. . . . But both winters were very severe, and probably the frost cracked the cement, and slates are so easily dislodged. It's not so bad in here. That's the advantage of a bricked floor. I'm afraid Mr Genge did not quite prepare you for it. The truth is, he has been so extremely busy, and labour and materials are so hard to get just now, and . . .'

Perfectly inattentive, Miss Ensor burst into tears, uttering the loud crowing sobs of second childhood. Snorting and sobbing, she swept past Mr Brown and his clean handkerchief and his red compassionate face, and went weeping through her ruined house, and out into the glaring sunlight.

'Look! Oh, the *poor* old thing!'

Both ladies leaped from the car and hurried to Miss Ensor.

'No wonder you're upset. It's the shock, isn't it? So frightful, seeing one's home devastated, everything gone in a minute. I do feel for you so frightfully. We both do. I suppose you've lived here quite a long time? That makes it worse, doesn't it?'

Now, while the first lady was patting Miss Ensor, the second lady looked up into the blue sky and exclaimed:

'Brutes! Inhuman brutes!'

'My God, yes! Still, I suppose it's some comfort to think we are doing it to them now. But that won't put your poor house back, will it? We are so sorry for you, you know. It's ghastly, just ghastly! But I'm sure you mustn't cry like this. Can't we take you somewhere and give you a nice cup of tea? That's what you want. Something to pull you together. You'll feel better then. Really, you will. Do come with us, we can all get introduced on the way to tea. After all, there's no room for all that nonsense in wartime, is there? That's one comfort, it has brought us all together in such a rational way.'

'Another comfort,' said the second lady, 'is that it only got the house, not you. That sort of comfort grows on one, I assure you. I *do* know, because my own poor little flat was torn to ribbons; and if I'd been able to get a taxi I'd have been back in it, and in ribbons, too. After all, life means a lot, doesn't it?'

'Oh, it certainly does,' rejoined the first lady. 'And everyone's being so marvellously brave. Think of all those poor souls in the East End, how splendid they all were. And I'm sure you're going to be just like them after you've had that cup of tea. And then you can tell us all about it. Was it a night raid or a daylight?'

This time they paused, and Miss Ensor could speak.

'It wasn't either. It was thirty-five billeted soldiers. And two hard winters. And some evacuated children. So I understand. And a vilely incompetent and dishonest house agent. There he is. You'd better ask him.'

The two ladies looked incuriously at Mr Brown, and looked away again.

'Oh, I say. What rotten luck! Really, it looks just as if a bomb had got it.'

After her furious speech Miss Ensor was again in tears.

'Poor old soul!'

'Of course, billeting can be the very devil. Did I tell you about Badger's billiard room?'

'He did. Still, one gets compensation, doesn't one?'

'Oh, yes. All that's seen to. A bit slow, of course, but wizard when it comes.'

'Well, you can't expect the poor old War Office to turn themselves into walruses and carpenters, can you? After all, they've got to win the war. But they always pay up in the end.'

'Oh, yes, they pay all right. Ultimately. There's nothing to worry about.'

Raising her voice, she repeated the words, and added:

'You're sure you won't come and have some tea? But I dare say you want to have a heart-to-heart with your house agent, so we won't take up any more of your time. But do cheer up, won't you? I'm sure everything will turn out much better than you think. It's only a question of time.'

The second lady added her plea that Miss Ensor should cheer up and remember that it might have been a bomb. And acknowledging Mr Brown's rigid glare with rigid inattention both ladies stepped into the car and drove away.

After a while Miss Ensor began to weep less violently, and presently to sob only, and then only to hiccough. In a rather hen-like way she began to tweak up groundsel from a vaguely-distinguishable circular flower bed. Mr Brown, sighing heavily, began to pull up groundsel too. But seeing her pause, and look at him with fury, he said:

'I'm afraid we ought to be getting back. That is, if you have been here long enough, and don't mind.'

THE TRUMPET SHALL SOUND

c. April 1942

No doubt, thought Mrs Mullen, looking at her niece, no doubt at all, everything was made uncommonly easy for these young ones, not like it was in her time. *Then* you didn't have a death in the house without knowing it.

Rightly speaking, you couldn't call this a death in the house; for poor old Dick, falling over a bicycle in the black-out, had been taken to the hospital, and in the hospital he had died; and from the hospital, no better than a parcel, he had been taken to the undertaker's place to await, no better than a parcel, the day of the funeral.

Flowers c/o Messrs Kedge, Ring St. Lower Town.

That is why the house felt so queer. No corpse in it, no black weight at its centre to keep it steady. No reason to step softly, no door with silence behind it. Not even the blinds drawn.

The spring sunshine shone full into the front room. There was a fire burning too, the room was very warm. But Cathie kept on shivering and pulling up the collar of her coat. Not tired enough, thought Mrs Mullen. If Dick had been brought home to die, the nursing and the running about and the sitting up and one thing and another would have knocked the nerves and the shivers out of her, left her in the right frame of mind to appreciate the repose of a funeral. These young women who thought they were making things so much easier for themselves, small families, bakers' bread, nowadays not even the whites boiled, were making a great mistake. If you'd got to be a woman it was better to be an old-fashioned woman, with plenty of work to keep your mind off it.

Cathie sat on the sofa, and beside her sat Gwennie, Dick's sister-in-law, and Gwennie's girl, Ramona. Ramona yawned incessantly. She was working in munitions, and this week was a night turn.

Soon we shall all be yawning, thought Mrs Mullen. She glanced at the clock. There was still some time to run before the car came for them.

By the window sat Freda, Mrs Mullen's unmarried sister, and Reg, Cathie's husband. He had got leave for his father-in-law's funeral. He sat on a small chair, leaning forward, with his hands dangling between his knees. Beside him stood the boy, Alan, staring at his shoulder badge and corporal's stripes, and slowly drawing them on the air with his forefinger.

'There would have been time for a cup of tea,' said Cathie.

'There's time now,' said Reg. 'I'll go and put on the kettle.'

'Don't trouble for me,' said Freda.

'Nor me, either. Six cups. That wouldn't leave much of Cathie's ration. Ah, you'll miss your poor old dad's ration, won't you, Cath? It'll make a difference.'

'I had a nice cup of tea on my way here,' said Freda. 'Between the buses.'

‘How long did it take you to come?’

‘Matter of three hours. They’ve taken off the Kitley bus, so now you have to go round by Swopham. And who do you think I met on the bus, Lottie? Old Mr Tanner, who used to keep the fish shop. You’ve never seen a man so changed.’

‘Well, he must be getting on, mustn’t he?’

‘Sixty-seven. You remember how rheumatic he was, and how he always wore a hat because of his face-ache? There he was, strolling into the bus bare-headed, with a potted flower under his arm. Why, Mr Tanner, I said, this war seems to be agreeing with you. And he told me he hasn’t had a twinge for the last ten years, and all because of wearing iodine socks. He was right sorry when I told him about poor Dick.’

‘Iodine socks? Yes, you do hear of them. All I know is, they never did anything for Florence Gander, Florence Toogood that was. Still, *she’s* constitutional. You remember Florence, don’t you, Gwennie? One time it looked as though she were going to marry poor old Dick.’

‘Didn’t she sing, or something?’

‘Sing or something?’ Mrs Mullen’s voice expressed reproachful surprise. ‘Why, she played on the violin, and passed examinations for it up in London. That’s how Dick took up with your sister. For in the last war Florence went round with a concert party, all in a bus together, called The Five Lucky Beans, or something, and Dick, he was in the army, of course, and the first time he came back on leave, “What’s become of Florence?” he said, and mother said, “Why, haven’t the girls told you about her engagement?” meaning the concert party. But just then the maroons went off and there was that awful Zeppelin, and so Florence went clean out of our heads, and Dick thought she'd taken up with some other boy, and when he came back next he got engaged to your Jessie, and Florence married Nut Gander. Just a misunderstanding, you see. Five children she had, one after another, and not a note of music among them. It's funny how things turn out.'

'Mum,' said the child. 'I think I'll just feed my rabbits.'

'I'll go with him,' said Reg, rising with alacrity.

Cathie looked as though she were about to speak, but said nothing. The three aunts exchanged glances, and then settled down more easily.

'Do you remember Buster, Lottie? And the day he took round the collecting bag at chapel in that blue suit of his? Lord, what a look he gave me as he went up the aisle! Impudent? He was worse than the seven monkeys.'

'And all the time he'd got two wives, one in Chelmsford and the other somewhere in Wales. Well, I don't mind admitting it now, the day that news came out I cried my eyes sore.'

'Yes, and you weren't the only one, either. And it wasn't only us girls that took on about it. Mrs Blandamer, George Blandamer's wife, who got up the whist-drives and socials – well, Julia Kinnear told me that she swallowed half a bottle of disinfectant, and only didn't die of it because they'd happened to eat some bad fish the evening before, and the fish and the disinfectant all came back together.'

'Yes, I heard something about that, too. Well, they do say, lucky at cards, unlucky in love. What about George, though?'

'Oh, all *he* ever knew of it was the fish.'

Ramona had shut her eyes and begun to breathe heavily. Now she slumped forward. Cathie put an arm about her, and settled the sleeping head on her shoulder. Her face lost its look of nervous strain as the sleeping girl's warmth invaded her.

'I should like a bit of tinned salmon, though. I haven't seen a tin for months,' said Freda.

'Ah, you should have bought it and put it by,' said Lottie Mullen. 'Hoarding or no hoarding, a person's got to keep even with the future. I don't mind telling you, if Lord Woolton were to come along and look under my old double bed he'd see more than the chamber.'

'In reason, I grant you.' Gwennie eased her scantily-cut black skirt over her knees. 'But the way some people behave, it's a scandal. You know Mrs Mortus, whose Irene works along with our Ramona? Well, last Thursday week I saw her get half a pound of biscuits in a queue, and then go back to the tail of the queue, and take off her glasses, and work her way up and get another half-pound. Well, I said to myself, now I suppose you'll go back again and take out your teeth. Oh, it makes my blood boil!'

'Yes, it makes one want to say something, doesn't it? But talking of bare-faced cheating, what about . . .'

'Mum! Mum!'

The child ran in, flourishing his cap.

'The car's outside, Mum. It's waiting for us.'

'Good Lord! And we were so happy talking over old times, we never heard it. Dear, dear! Poor Dick. Not even brought back for as much as to come in and go out again. It doesn't seem quite reverent, does it, to go out of a house for a funeral with no corpse going before. Where's my gloves?'

The undertaker's car was old and stately, so roomy that it held them all. Reg and the boy sat in front, where Reg and the driver conversed in undertones about double declutching. Cathie and Ramona still clung to each other, and the aunts, ennobled by the deep springing and all the little amber knobs, sat silent and upright, glancing at the shabby streets as though a Jug and Bottle entrance meant nothing to them.

Outside Mr Kedge's establishment the hearse was waiting, the four mutes standing beside it. As they neared, the mutes scrambled up and it moved off. Another car which had been waiting swung out to follow theirs.

'Well, my goodness, whoever's that? Cathie! Who's in that other car?'

'I didn't see.'

'Well, surely, you ought to know. People don't follow a body uninvited. Here, Gwennie, you're the limberest among us. You watch out of this back window and see who it is.'

'It's the Blackbones. Fred and Mary and old Dodger Blackbone.'

'*The Blackbones*? Well!'

'The Blackbones?'

'Gwennie! Look again. It can't be the Blackbones.'

'Yes, it is. And in mourning, too, as far as one can see.'

'I've never heard of such a thing. After the way Mrs Dodger walked off with our Aunt Mabel's furniture, and Dick never getting as much as a teaspoon, and all of us knowing he was her favourite nephew. Cathie! What are those Blackbones doing at your father's funeral?'

'Well, I suppose they are coming too, Aunt Lot.'

'My word! And is that all you can do about it?'

'Well, what can I do?'

'Did you know they were coming?'

Ramona came stare-eyed and assertive out of her doze.

'Why shouldn't they come, Mrs Mullen? It's Uncle Dick's funeral, I suppose.'

'Hush, Ramona dear.'

'Uncle Dick's funeral? That's just what I'm complaining of. If Dodger wants to go to a funeral, I should think he could pick out some other funeral where he'd be more in keeping. Or wait for his own. Why, it would make Dick turn in his grave.'

Cathie preserved an unassenting silence. Ramona yawned with deliberation. Gwennie, her face mottled with blushes, looked steadily out of the window.

'Well, wouldn't it? After the way Dodger treated your Dad?'

'Dad and Cousin Randall got on all right, Aunt Lot.'

'D'you mean to say . . .?'

'They used to meet at the Buffaloes, and Cousin Randall was very fond of Dad.'

The car drew up before the church. The coffin was lifted out, the clergyman came from the porch to meet it.

'*I am the Resurrection . . .*'

When he began to speak it was obvious that his teeth were false and didn't fit. On every sibilant he sounded a shrill whistle.

'Who on earth's this awful old parson?' whispered Mrs Mullen, as she and Freda, Cathie, Reg, and the boy, came up from their knees in the front pew. 'Why haven't you got Mr Dacre?'

'He's gone to be an army chaplain, Aunt Lot.'

A little farther down on the opposite side of the aisle sat the Blackbones. Freda, who had no dignity, kept twisting herself to look at them. Mrs Mullen continued to look steadfastly before her, where the coffin, mounted on trestles, seemed irreconcilably large and dominating for anything representing Dick. In the pew just behind Gwennie was freely and comfortably weeping.

Well, perhaps the coffin was in the right of it. Perhaps her impression of Dick was a false one, after all. For one can't be sure, even about one's own brother. Dick had been reconciled with Dodger. For years he had been meeting Dodger at the Buffaloes, going round to the pub with him afterwards, talking to him of carrier pigeons and tomato blight. Her own brother – and she had never so much as suspected it.

Staring at the coffin, so aloof and so imminent, Mrs Mullen was penetrated by a realisation of the vanity of this world. What's the use, she thought to herself, what's the use of sticking up for one's principles, what's the use of getting up into one's best corsets to attend a funeral, why pay burial insurance, why have wars? There, across the aisle, was Dodger, grown old in wickedness, and here was she, worn out with keeping respectable. And to that whistling clergyman there, not a pin to choose between them. Just two elderly persons who would soon be funerals, and the only odds, which happened to come first.

A lot of good horse sense would be buried with her. And Dodger, he'd take more knowledge of the world than he was born with down into the grave with him. But nobody would dig for it, nobody wanted the wisdom of the old, any more than they wanted those big mahogany sideboards. That sideboard of Aunt Mabel's, and the dumb waiter, and the eight chairs, so solid you could hardly lift them: Dodger had got them, and Mrs Dodger had dusted them; but young Mrs Fred would sell them as soon as Dodger had hopped it.

'*For the trumpet shwee! – all shwee! – ound . . .*'

But had Saint Paul, thought the Reverend Mr Amwood, foreseen these funeral countenances, blankly unconvinced, glumly polite, amid this funeral incense of dying flowers and mothballs? And with which mourners had Mr Kedge, thriftily complying with the petrol restrictions, ordained that he should ride to the cemetery? Saint Paul, *in watchings often, in fastings often, in stripes above measure, in prisons more frequent, in deaths oft,* had not been required to take over, in his old age, the duty of an industrial parish, under a most energetic and uncongenial Bishop, and on a heavy clay soil.

'*Therefore, my beloved brethren, be ye steadfast, unmovable, always abounding in the work of the Lord, forasmuch as ye know that your labour is not in vain in the Lord.*'

The coffin was lifted and carried from the church. Mr Kedge approached the clergyman.

'Well!' exclaimed Freda. 'If those Blackbones aren't taking the parson with them! What next? I've a good mind to fetch him out again.'

'Do let be, Freda,' said Mrs Mullen. 'And try to remember that this is a funeral, not a remnant sale.'

'Always did fight like cats, those two,' whispered Gwennie to her daughter.

It was a long way to the cemetery, and they drove in silence, except once, when Lottie Mullen, driven to speak her thought aloud, said heavily: 'What's the use?' Then they looked at her enquiringly; but as each left it to the other to take up the question, no one answered.

The cemetery lay on the outskirts of the town, rising above the sad slow river, the countless identical ridges of slate-roofed artisan dwellings, the factories and warehouses. It was a newish cemetery, the further half of it lay unused, the trees planted by the Town Council still had a youthful tender look. So many of the graves had bunches of daffodils on them that the cemetery appeared to be twinkling with daffodils and responding with yellow flashes to the April sunlight. Two other funerals were taking place. They seemed very small and unimportant among the expanse of completed graves.

Shining, too, in the April sunlight the coffin on its six black legs proceeded like some queer quadruped, turning first right, then left, as though unerringly nosing out its lair. The newly-dug clay, heaped up, was yellow and shiny like the coffin, the walls of the grave had an ochreous glister. The gravedigger was standing a little aloofly behind a neighbouring headstone.

Up shuffled Dodger, his boots creaking. His face was pinched, his few locks of grey hair lifted in the wind. Not long for this world, thought Mrs Mullen. No wonder he's having a good look. Raising his eyes from the open grave Dodger's glance met hers. Still vibrating to thoughts of mortality she tried to convey by her expression that the past was being overlooked. Dodger blinked once or twice, and turned away.

Up here above the town the wind was blowing quite briskly. White clouds raced over the blue, the daffodils wagged, the clergyman's surplice rustled as he stood waiting while the bearers lifted the wreaths from the coffin, and the mourners took their places. Freda was having trouble with her hat. Once it almost blew off, and Mr Kedge sprang forward, noiseless as a shadow, to retrieve it.

How tiresome Freda was, always a fidget, always coming to bits just like her own parcels. And there was that girl Ramona, looking at her so sarcastically, and Mary Blackbone ostentatiously not noticing. Why must such unpleasantness mar the funeral, just at the most solemn moment, too? But the outdoor part of a funeral usually went wrong: at Hilda's funeral George had had a fit, at George's funeral the wasps were something chronic. If only that clergyman would begin!

He began. Under the heavy rhythm of the burial sentences everything subsided into order and a dreamy majesty, except his own surplice, in which the wind now made a most extraordinary drumming and fluster. Suddenly the gravedigger jumped out from behind his headstone, waving his arms, and shouting:

'Look up there! Look out!'

His voice ripped through the ceremony. They looked. He was pointing to the sky. There, just coming out of a cloud, was something like an enormous pale bird with beating wings.

Dangling from it, as the mouse dangles from the claws of the white owl, was a dark object. Now that they looked the noise of the beating parachute, the drumming and flustering, seemed overwhelmingly loud. The noise grew louder, the thing came lower.

Reg seized Alan, and dropped him into the grave. Then he grabbed Cathie, and dropped her in beside the child.

'Jump in, jump in! It's a landmine coming down.'

One after another the mourners got into the grave. The mutes came to the edge, hesitated, seemed inclined to follow. Mr Kedge, with a recalling gesture, pointed them to some bushes. Remembering their position they retired there, and lay down. The clergyman still remained standing. Mr Kedge touched his elbow, pointed to the grave. The clergyman, on such an occasion, would rank as one of the family. But Mr Amwood shook his head. The parachute came lower, reeling and billowing. It seemed to fill the whole sky. Pursing his lips, Mr Kedge lay down also.

There seemed to be no end to the waiting. Away in the town an engine blew off steam, and one could hear the birds singing. Meanwhile Mr Amwood had knelt down at the graveside and was whistling through the commendatory prayer for the dying. Dodger, pressed close and bony to Lottie Mullen, commented in her ear:

'Bit previous, isn't he, giving us all up for lost like that?'

His pale wrinkled face was lit with an expression of indomitable craft and assurance.

'Amen,' said Mr Amwood rapidly, snatched out his teeth, and cast himself down face forward.

There was a crash that swelled into a long roar. The mourners in the grave were thrown pell-mell against each other. The breath of life seemed to be dragged out of them, they gasped and choked. The air became darkened by a cloud of dust, in which dead leaves, pebbles, twigs, daffodils, clods of earth, shreds of stuff and paper, fragments of wood and stone and metal, were suspended. Glancing into the spattered darkness Mrs Mullen saw two funeral wreaths, her own and Gwennie's, rise up, hang twirling, and fall dishevelled into the grave.

At last, into this darkened air, they saw Mr Amwood erect himself, tall and ghostly-white, saying:

'You may come out now.'

Aided by shoves from Fred and Reg they scrambled out, and looked around. The coffin was lying on its side. Near it was a large fragment of marble, lettered *Also Emma*, and Mr Kedge was holding a bloodstained handkerchief to his ear, and saying it was a near go. Everything was covered with dust and rubble. At the western end of the cemetery a column of dust was still boiling up, and beneath it some small figures were scurrying to and fro.

The funeral proceeded. The coffin was lowered into the grave, earth was scattered on it, and the last prayers were said. Walking rather unsteadily the party turned away. It was then that Dodger went up to Mrs Mullen, remarking affably:

'Hullo, Lot. Looked as though we might be spending the night here, didn't it?'

She gave him an unmoving full-face glare, and walked on.

'Well,' said Gwennie, walking beside her. 'I'll tell you this. I'll be more than thankful to sit down. I never heard any aeroplane, did you?'

Providential, Mrs Mullen was thinking. Providential. If it hadn't been for that landmine, like as not I'd still be forgiving Dodger. And leaving him my best teaset, I dare say, to show bygones were bygones. And all just because of coming over so soft in church, giving way to the funeral, and thinking *Poor old Dodger*! That's what funerals do, if one's not on one's guard. And Dodger as ready to get round me as a terrier round a rat.

'I heard one thing,' she said, 'and that's what Dodger Blackbone said to me in the grave. All those Blackbones tumbling in without so much as a by-your-leave, and Mr Kedge and that poor old parson left to perish on the brink. Trust Dodger! Trust him to find a safe place to start blaspheming in! Dodger by name, and Dodger by nature.'

'What did Dodger say?'

'I could no more bring myself to forgive it,' said Lottie Mullen, 'than I could bring myself to repeat it. Not if it was my dying hour.'

She strode on firmly towards the cemetery gates.

SCORCHED EARTH POLICY

18 April 1942

Colonel Edmund Pomeroy (retired) and his wife, Dollie, lived in the wilds of Huntingdonshire, where the descendants of Cromwell's Ironsides go proudly to chapel and leave the Church of England to strangers, families disgraced by bankruptcy or bastardy, and the gentry, and where the landscape rises and falls in the slow rollers of a clay soil.

It is an elm-tree soil. And now, in the third spring of war, the elms that took so much goodness out of the ground were shedding their blooms, and the Pomeroys' goats were spitting them out and complaining fastidiously.

The Colonel's face, as he stooped seriously above the onion bed, suddenly cracked open in a grin. 'Why, good Lord! Those goats will do it for us,' he said. 'What a fool I was to overlook the goats! Dollie! All we need do about destroying the garden is to shut up the goats in it.'

'Not shoot them?' She was halfway up a ladder, pruning an apple tree. The words, spoken in a piping treble, floated down like some odd bird song.

'Not I!' said the Colonel with decision. 'Four live goats

running loose, and one of them that damned Selina of yours, would be as good as a band of guerrillas any day. No, no! It would be short-sighted to shoot the goats. I bet those Russians would never shoot Selina.'

'What about the potatoes, though? We have enough to last all through the summer.'

'Potatoes? Easy. They just go into the pond. What a mercy, I say, that we never got round to draining that pond!'

'Or we could pour paraffin on them.'

'Mustn't waste paraffin. We shall want all the paraffin we can spare for the hayrick.'

'I've sometimes felt rather uneasy about our store of paraffin,' Dollie said. 'It's seemed rather like hoarding. But I'm thankful now.'

'We shall need every drop of it,' said the Colonel. 'I wish to God we'd kept the car. Can't scorch anything with two bicycles.'

From the outset of the war the Pomeroys had set themselves to produce, to conserve, to economise. 'Bound to be a shortage of wood,' the Colonel had said, daubing Solignum on the framework of his black-out screens. 'Nails, too. Pick up those bent ones, my dear, and put 'em in a box, and I'll straighten 'em later.'

'About those damsons,' his wife had said. 'I'm going to dry them. I shall want all the sugar I can save for extra marmalade.'

No shortage found the Pomeroys unforeseeing. When onions vanished, 'First Prize, Bunch of Leeks, Presented by Colonel Pomeroy' enriched every local whist drive held for a good cause. When oranges disappeared, the biscuits at the Evacuee Children's Christmas Tea were flavoured with Mrs Pomeroy's dried-and-pounded orange peel. When wrapping paper was discontinued, string bags, made by Colonel Pomeroy in his spare time from oddments of string collected by Mrs Pomeroy, were sold for the Red Cross. They raised mushrooms in their air raid shelter, lettuces among their roses, potatoes on their lawn. Producing, saving, conserving – what else was there, they said, for two septuagenarian fogies living in the wilds to do? Naturally, Mrs Pomeroy found herself in charge of a salvage dump, where, during hot weather, she put on her gas mask (for there is a use for everything, even gas masks) and sorted old bones. Inevitably, Colonel Pomeroy became an air raid warden, and a Home Guard, and a billeting officer, and heroically paraded on occasions of local pageantry with an armband lettered 'BO'. But these were by-activities. Wartime economy was their daily bread.

As war and economy went on, the Pomeroys' hoards and contrivances filled the house. But still there was a place for everything – for tin foil, and corks, and empty cotton reels, and rubber bands, and heeltaps of soap, and tobacco pried from cigarette stubs, and sawdust, and shavings, and razor blades, and dandelion roots (coffee), and cinders, and old felt hats that could be made into bedroom slippers; the Colonel's frame for making camouflage nets fitted quite well into the bathroom, the airing cupboard was excellent for drying mushrooms and raising seedlings in, and when Mrs Pomeroy had filled every jam pot and pickle jar, she began filling a collection of Grecian urns bequeathed by an aunt. Everything was so neatly arranged that the general effect was merely one of a more extensive neatness; and amid all their economies the Pomeroys contrived to go on improving their pocket-handkerchief property, the Colonel making new shelves and cupboards out of packing cases and Mrs Pomeroy sewing new patchwork coats for the chairs and sofas, and both of them uniting to rebuild the dilapidated summer house as a goat shed.

'It seems a pity that we can't use Selina indoors too,' continued the Colonel.

'I've got the inside of the house pretty well planned,' Dollie said. 'Once you've got a bonfire going, I shall bring out the sheets and the blankets. The mattresses are rather a problem, but I shall do what I can with the air raid hatchet and then upset the sand and water buckets over the remains. As for the pillows, I thought I'd shove some of the feathers down the toilet, to block the drains. Boots and shoes can go into that invaluable pond. I thought you'd see to that while I was ripping up the clothes. Then there's all the food. It seemed to me that I might very well begin by emptying some treacle into the salted beans, and the parsnip wine can go into the pickled-cabbage tub, along with the soap. Things like flour and tea and oatmeal – they're no trouble. Just skirmish them about on the floor. Then, while you're smashing the canned stuff, I deal with the jam and maybe just frisk through the china cupboard. Do you remember that sideshow there used to be at fairs – a dresserful of cheap crockery and twopence a shy? Breaking Up the Home, it was called.'

'The secret is to aim at the shelf,' the Colonel said. 'People aim at the china. You'll see nine out of ten make that mistake. But a good aim at the shelf – that's what brings 'em down.'

'How to scorch the coal cellar – that beats me. This wartime coal – '

'Leave the coal, my dear, and wish 'em joy of it.'

'What will you do about all your lovely tools?'

'Pond,' the Colonel said firmly. 'They go in first of all. Except the hammer, for dealing with the windows and doors and so forth. Damn these weeds. Beginning to come up all over the place.' He went stiffly down on his knees, saying that it needed hoeing, really.

'I'm so sorry,' Dollie said. 'I meant to weed this morning. But the jelly took longer than I meant. Six pots.'

'Hm, that's not bad. Sugar still holding out?'

'Mary Amstice is letting me have three pounds of hers as a swap for tomato ketchup. Jack, I've had an idea! Can't we burst the boiler?'

'Eh?'

'If we let all the water run out and then stoke up the fire and get it nicely roaring just before we leave. That would burst the boiler, wouldn't it? It does at Christmas, in frozen homes. Yes, and that would solve the saucepans, too. We could leave them on the hot plate, empty, to burn their bottoms out.'

'That's a very good idea, Dollie. A damn good idea. And while you're about it, you might remember to burn my flute. I'll be damned if they go breathing down my flute.' He rose. 'What about some tea?'

They walked toward the house, neat as a toy below the elm trees. The kitchen window was open and on the sill stood six pots of jelly. In the afternoon stillness they could hear the fluttering breath of the kettle, just coming to a boil.

The Colonel began to whistle softly. Lightly, Mrs Pomeroy put her hand on his arm, her small, horny hand, smelling of fruit and of earth. They turned and looked back over the garden. But their scrutiny did not remain there. They stared at the empty, rolling landscape, at the calm sky, as though searching for a signal that would release them, after the years of saving and conserving and piecemeal prudence, into the positiveness of destruction.

THE FAMILY REVIVED

11 July 1942

'Speaking for myself,' said Mrs Bogle, 'I believe that this fuel-rationing scheme has been *planned*.'

The Canadian pilot who was spending his leave with the Killdews (Sir Ludovick and Lady Killdew had relatives in Canada) looked up, startled. He was a polite young man, so polite that he was now attending Mrs Bogle's Sunday Salvage Afternoon and slicing metal butts off old cartridge cases with the rest of us in our Dorsetshire cottage, but stirring behind his politeness, as a deer stirs in a thicket, was a regretful conviction that the English are given over to cynicism and levity, and here was further proof of it. The rest of us, who know Mrs Bogle better, understood that she was not speaking of Sir William Beveridge and the Secretary for Mines but of that somewhat jesuitical agency which she refers to as A Power for Good or Something Behind It All.

'Because of family life,' she continued. 'For think how it will draw us together! The whole family sitting round the fire, just like the old days, you know, when roasted crabs hiss in the bowl.'

'Sounds like cruelty to animals to me,' remarked Miss Webb, the land girl, in an undertone.

In an undertone, Mrs Bogle replied, 'No, Shakespeare.'

'Considered in that light,' said Mrs Larpent, 'I call it belated. Of course, all plans are, except possibly layettes, and one's usually behindhand with them. How can fuel rationing revive family life when none of us has any family left? I can't believe that the hissing of a roasted crab, or the drowning of a parson's saw, either, come to that –'

'More Shakespeare,' Mrs Bogle said, patting Miss Webb's knee soothingly.

'– is likely to lure Bill back from Iceland,' Mrs Larpent continued, 'and Susan from Dover, and Isabel from Delhi, and the cook and housemaid from their factory. On the evenings when George isn't on ARP and I'm not washing up in the canteen, I suppose we shall sit by the fire in total silence. But we do that anyway.' She whetted her knife on the carborundum and took up another cartridge case.

'I've never been able to understand why one talks of sitting *round* a fire,' observed Miss Pilgrim. 'At the best, one can only sit hemispherically.'

Speaking together, the Canadian said, 'Campfires,' and George Larpent said, 'A survival from the great hall of the Middle Ages, when the fire was in the middle of the room and the smoke went out by the roof.'

'Really?' Mrs Bogle tossed a handful of metal butts into the tray for waste cardboard. 'How interesting! And it does quite as well for an oil heater, doesn't it?'

Delighted with this further revelation of Something

Behind It All, she continued with vigour, 'Besides, why need it be only one family? It might be two or three. Because, of course, what Mrs Larpent says is perfectly true. None of us can call our families our own just now. But if we took turns spending the evening together – those of us that have evenings – we'd be keeping up the tradition of family life, wouldn't we? And think of the saving! Why don't we plan out our fireside rota here and now?'

There was an evasive pause, broken by Miss Pilgrim saying, 'People in the East burn cow dung, don't they?'

'We did ourselves last winter,' said Lady Killdew. 'It gives a splendid glow once it's kindled.'

'The glow,' said her husband, 'doesn't last.'

'Personally,' said Mrs Larpent, 'I have been thinking deeply about the Venetian custom of wearing a farthingale and having a little charcoal brazier underneath it and a devoted follower to puff the brazier.'

'Oh, my dear,' said Mrs Bogle, 'I'm afraid you will be disappointed. It's almost impossible to get charcoal.'

'In the last war,' said Miss Webb, 'my mother one day was in a train, going from Ely to Scarborough, and it was winter, and the train wasn't heated. And then a man got in, and after he'd settled down he produced two lengths of rubber gas piping. And he put the top ends into his mouth, and tucked the bottom ends into his boots, and began to breathe. After a bit he noticed my mother noticing him, and he took out the two bits of piping and explained that he suffered terribly from cold feet, but by breathing into his boots he kept them quite cozy. He was a commercial traveller.'

'Well, that was practical,' said the Canadian.

'Not in this war!' cried Mrs Bogle. 'Rubber, you know. Really, my plan is much the best. We must share our firesides. And I'm going to suggest that you all come to us every Monday and Thursday. We shall have our work, you know, and the wireless going, and perhaps Sir Ludovick would read aloud – one never seems to get much reading done in wartime. And we could talk over our various problems. There is always so much to talk about. Or would Tuesdays be better than Mondays? We could eat roast chestnuts, and –' Here she caught sight of Mr Bogle approaching the table. 'Oh, Hereward! You're just in time to hear what we are planning for next winter, such a delightful scheme for saving fuel. We're all going to . . .'

Meanwhile, Mr Bogle, a large man moving with extraordinary stealthiness and speed, had attained his objective and was saying to the Canadian, 'You're the fellow I need. Just walk round the garden with me, will you? I want some advice about felling a few trees.'

'I don't know much about trees,' said the Canadian. 'My family lived in an apartment house.' But he rose obediently, for he was a very polite young man.

'Trees, Hereward?' Mrs Bogle said. 'Surely you're not going to cut down any of my dear trees? Not the old crab apple – so mossy! *Not* the Spanish chestnut, for we are just planning how we shall roast chestnuts when we are all sitting together reviving the family!'

'Must grow more food,' said Mr Bogle. 'Besides, logs may come in handy.'

'But Hereward, both the kitchen stove and the sitting room grate are too small for logs. We discovered that last winter, and you know how tired you got of carving them smaller.'

'The study grate isn't,' said he, and speedily, stealthily retired, taking the Canadian with him.

Mrs Bogle flushed, and the sudden colour and the round-eyed, wondering stare that watched the fading-away of another illusion made her look momentarily young again. And each one of us, I suppose, condemned the churlish Bogle and hoped that nice young Canadian, the soul of chivalry, might be kicking him outside in the shrubbery. There was a hush, but necessarily it had to be brief, and before Mrs Bogle's predatory good intentions could revive, Lady Killdew said to Mrs Larpent, 'Lucy, dear, there's one thing we *must* talk over before we go home. When are we having our Drive for Bones?'

THE MOTHERS

1 August 1942

The children of England get their primary schooling either in national schools or church schools. Only a blind man could remain unaware that the school at Long Twizzel was a church school – and he, if he got inside it, would have known by the smell, which was vaulted, mouldy, and gothic. It was a very small building with an inordinately high-pitched roof. Over the peaked porch was engraved, in curly figures, 1859. Inside, high above the chimney piece and the rusty stove chimney, was a faded watercolour portrait of a young man in Hussar's uniform, and under the portrait was painted in letters equally curly: D C H 1833-1855. *Christo in pauperibus suis.*

For years the watercolour Hussar had been no more than a variant of the school walls, like the lancet windows, and the map of the world with British possessions coloured pink. The windows were cobwebbed, the map was fly-blown, the young man was faded. They were all educational, all of a piece. But in September 1939 Mrs Pitcher began to tell the class how the young man, full of virtue and gallantry, had died for his country fighting the Russians, that he was young Mr Dewhurst

Charles Hunter, and that the sorrowing Hunter family had built the school in his memory. This revived his colours. Every child in the village knew Sir Charles and Lady Hunter, who came to Long Twizzel every autumn and shot partridges – though with no perceptible sorrow for a soldier son.

Mrs Pitcher herself was another demonstration that the school was a church school. She was a middle-aged woman with an anxious, contentious face and a bilious complexion. Every line of her body, every note in her voice, registered superiority and how painfully superiority is attained and preserved. She had a crippled husband, who cleaned the church. It was also rumoured that he cleaned for Mrs Pitcher, and cooked their midday dinner – a fact, if true, equally disgraceful to himself and to his wife.

To be so superior, to have so many sick headaches and a husband who cooked for her, added to Mrs Pitcher's statutory unpopularity as village schoolmistress. Mrs Mutley, Mrs Bing, Mrs Alsop, and Mrs Bert Hawkins – whose maternity provided a steady quota of the Long Twizzel school attendance – were always on the lookout for further reasons to dislike Mrs Pitcher. Now, to her affectedly small consumption of beef sausages, her stuck-up airs at Holy Communion, her nonsense about birds-nesting, and her old rainproof, the war added a series of rousing new grievances. War was no sooner declared than Mrs Pitcher started putting ideas into the children's heads. She told them about the bombing of Warsaw, and the shooting of Polish civilians. She told them of hospitals burning and children starving. She told them about submarines and food supplies, and made them wear their gas masks for half an hour every Monday. When she started to tell them about German concentration camps and the persecution of the Jews it was felt that these outrages had gone far enough. A deputation of mothers, sullenly mumbling, called upon Canon Dimple, and Canon Dimple called upon Mrs Pitcher.

'One must remember, Mrs Pitcher, that these are simple country children. They are not likely to come in contact with these horrors.'

'That is why I thought they ought to hear about them. If we are in the war, they should know it.'

'Surely, surely! Of course we must all take our part in the struggle. For instance, there are the special prayers. You use them, do you not?'

'Every morning.'

'Excellent, excellent! Then I have been thinking that it would be good to set up a School National Savings effort. *That* is a campaign in which we can all share.'

'Several of the children are buying savings stamps already. But do you think that's enough?'

'Well, every little helps. And later on, no doubt, there will be other openings for service. The farmers, for instance, will certainly need occasional labour. And for the rest I venture to suggest that it will be wisest to concentrate on the British effort. After all, Mrs Pitcher, we are British first and foremost. Well, I suppose we must soon be thinking about Christmas decorations. *Good* afternoon, Mrs Pitcher.'

Concentrating on the British effort, Mrs Pitcher soon afforded the village mothers another reason for dislike. She had two sons in the army, and both were non-commissioned officers.

'My son here and my son there, and sticking up bits from picture papers all over the place,' said Mrs Mutley. 'I suppose she thinks she owns the war.'

Pictures of Libya, pictures of India. In the autumn of 1941 the pictures of India were supplemented by pictures of Singapore. In January 1942 the pictures of Singapore had to be removed and their place filled by pictures of the United States – for, as Canon Dimple remarked, we are English-speaking first and foremost. The shadow of death is always a reconciler, and for some weeks after the fall of Singapore every mother in Long Twizzel, overlooking the past, was sedulous to enquire of Mrs Pitcher if she had heard anything about Sergeant Pitcher yet, if she expected to hear soon, if the strain was not terrible, and if it was not too awful to think of anyone being taken prisoner by those torturing little Japs; and in return Mrs Pitcher, more than ever ghastly with superiority and sick headaches, would speak with a rigid elegance about patriotism, sacrifice, and a willing endurance.

By the spring, of course, she was as briskly loathed as ever. Indeed, Mrs Pitcher was always particularly unpopular in spring because of Nature Study.

In spring it is the duty of every village schoolmistress to foster a love of nature and kindness to animals. While encouraging the children to gather wild flowers for the Easter church decorations, she must remind them not to uproot primroses and violets, or tear up bluebells, or break off boughs from fruit trees, or trespass into the Manor woods after daffodils. In spring too she must avail herself of young lambs and birds' nests as the ideal means of approach to a reverent understanding of biological processes, and also prevent the children from stealing birds' eggs, cutting the wings off fledglings, and throwing stones at valuable pedigree calves. For years Mrs Pitcher had hated spring. In spring her headaches were at their worst. In spring her chilblains broke. In spring the cuckoo came, and sang on and on, shouting her down as she led the school prayers and the recitations of the multiplication tables and 'The Lake Isle of Innisfree'. In spring the children were nothing but little nuisances; and the lambs and the birds were nothing but nuisances either – always provoking to sin, and not able to look after themselves.

In the spring of 1942 Mrs Pitcher realised with horror that a pair of swallows had chosen to build in the peaked porch.

'Shoo, shoo!' she exclaimed, waving her umbrella. 'Don't you build here, you silly creature!'

The mother swallow flashed past her, no more to be turned aside than a bullet.

There was nothing for it. On the morrow Mrs Pitcher gave the children a lesson on the swallow. The swallow, she said, is a migrant. Every spring swallows come to England in order to have their little ones, flying all the way from Africa, led by the most wonderful instinct (*and more fools they*). All through the summer we can see them catching flies, horrid little stinging flies, in order to feed their babies. And in autumn, warned by an instinct equally wonderful that there would be no more flies, they gather their young ones and fly back to Africa (*if they have survived to do it*).

'Africa's where the fighting is,' said Mona Mutley. 'I expects lots of swallows get killed there now, don't they, teacher?'

The swallow, with young ones to feed, catches more than twice its own weight of flies in a day, continued Mrs Pitcher. Every one loves the swallow, so clever, so harmless, and so useful, catching the flies that would otherwise become such a nuisance. Such wonderful little birds have had many beautiful poems written about them.

'Your other son's in Africa, isn't he, teacher?' said Ruby Bing.

On no account was the swallows' nest in the porch to be touched. Any child climbing up to finger it, or daring to steal one of the eggs, would get the cane. For they must all be proud that a mother swallow had chosen to build on the school, actually inside the porch. Next year the swallows, if not molested, would come again. And perhaps by then, said Mrs Pitcher, they will have seen a great British victory in Libya, and we shall be at peace.

The swallows' nest became an obsession with Mrs Pitcher. If the birds had been building in her stomach she could not have been more painfully aware of them. Above the yawns and the giggles and the scuffling feet and the droning voices of the class she heard the whirr of the swallows' flight and their twittered conversations. Steadfastly glaring at Bobbie Mutley or Irene Alsop she still saw their shadows flash past the window, momentarily flicking aside the steady beat of the sun. The plastered nest, the beam splashed with their droppings, the fragments of down that stuck to it – she knew it as well as her own parlour. And hearing the first squawks of the fledglings she began to sweat and tremble. Still the nest was untouched. She could not make out why. She had not noticed that the children realised – better than she, maybe – how jealously she watched over the nest in the porch, and so found it more convenient to go birds'-nesting along the hedges.

One wet Saturday she said to her husband that she reckoned the young swallows would be flying by midsummer. He looked up from his own preoccupation, and said:

'Looks like Tobruk will have fallen before midsummer, too. Why don't you think about your own flesh and blood for a change, instead of those bloody birds?'

His expression was so haggard and furious that she turned away and began to busy herself with the window geraniums. Suddenly, with a sort of bark she rushed out of the room.

In the school porch was Kenneth Fearon. Why him? she thought; he had always seemed a negligible creature, pale and dull and born to be bullied. He had thrown a rope over the beam and noosed it, and now was swarming up the rope. She caught him by the collar and swung him down.

'Now what are you up to? Are you after those swallows?'

He was silent, staring at the ground.

'Are you after those swallows, I say?'

He drooped before her. With the tip of a pale tongue he moistened his pale lips.

'Why can't you leave them alone? Don't you know it's wrong to take birds from the nest? Why, it's cruel! Think of the poor mother!'

Still he was silent.

'Do you hear what I say?'

He wriggled, and wrenched himself free. Scrabbling up handfuls of pebbles he began to stone the nest.

'I hate them! I hate them! I wish I had a gun, I'd shoot the lot. No, I wouldn't! I'd catch them and wring their heads off.'

The porch was full of his screams, his stampings, the noise of pebbles spattering against the beam. Suddenly the swallow flew in. Straight as a bullet she aimed herself at the nest, folded her wings, disappeared. A moment later the doorway was darkened by the shape of Mrs Fearon, panting violently.

'What are you doing to my Ken? I could hear him half across the village.'

'I shall have more to do to Kenneth,' replied Mrs Pitcher. 'He is a very naughty boy.'

'If you dare lay a finger on him . . . Look at his clean collar, all pulled about. Never you mind *her*, Ken. Come along with me, and shut up, do!'

'I hate you all!' he exclaimed; and escaping between them ran down the street.

The swallow flew out again, to hunt more food. The two women, their anger dashed by embarrassment and a kind of dismay, stood watching its flight, each glad to have an excuse not to look at each other. Smoothing back her wet red hair Mrs Fearon mumbled:

'Upsetting a child like that . . . Now he'll be sick, like as not.'

'You had better put him to bed,' said the schoolmistress coldly. She began to walk across to her house. Mrs Fearon unnoosed the rope, and followed her, looking like a frustrated hangman.

'Good afternoon, Mrs Pitcher. Good afternoon, Mrs Fearon. *What* a dreadful day!'

Composing themselves they turned and greeted Mrs Dimple.

'Still, I dare say the gardens need it. The Canon was saying that if it weren't for the hay he'd really have to pray for rain! I've just seen Kenneth, Mrs Fearon. So wet, poor child!'

'Oh!'

'Any more airgraph letters from your boy in Libya, Mrs Pitcher?'

'No.'

'Ah, well! Of course he's busy just now, isn't he? How lucky I am to meet you both! I'm just going round to explain to the members that our next Mothers' Union meeting will be on the twenty-first. The Canon is going to talk to us on Motherhood. Of course, you'll both come, won't you?'

ENGLAND, HOME AND BEAUTY

10 October 1942

Above the mantelpiece was a portrait of an English poet of the nineteenth century, a minor poet but sufficiently immortal for visitors to the Sillery household to feel a slight shock on learning that John Sillery had also been mortal enough to be Mr Sillery's grandfather. On the mantelpiece, which was long and wide, were most of the objects one expects to find on an English mantelpiece: some photographs, a stoneware jug holding pheasant tail feathers and another holding spills, a clock, a tobacco jar, a pair of Georgian silver candlesticks, a tortoiseshell box, and a bottle of dog medicine. In the grate, for it was summer, was an arrangement of fir cones, rather dusty. Before the hearth was an elderly Persian rug, and standing in the centre of the rug was a machine gun, mounted on its tripod and looking like a pet alligator.

In through the French windows came Mr Sillery and Major Puncheon, both of the village Home Guard, and a dozen women. The women were of various ages and various degrees, but all of them were flushed and most of them were out of breath. For few women are accustomed to throwing overhand,

and the Ladies' Shooting Class, having mastered the theory and practice of shooting with a rifle, had this afternoon gone on to a study of the hand grenade. Now twelve pairs of eyes were fixed beadily on the pet alligator.

'This,' said Mr Sillery, 'is a machine gun. It is set up ready for action.'

Mrs Dowling, whose neuritis was chronic, ceased to rub her forearm. She folded her arms and waited.

'And a very useful weapon, too,' added Major Puncheon.

'Which bit do you pull first?' enquired Mercy Hazard. She was flushed but not out of breath. The flush was partly pride. War had taken her three brothers, but not before they had seen to her education. Mercy's hand grenade had repeatedly gone over the bough of the walnut tree and, as a result, Mercy's hair was now hanging over her eyes. She pulled out a pocket comb and settled it, still gazing at the machine gun.

'We will begin with how to load it,' said Mr Sillery. 'This is the belt.' It passed from hand to hand, and Mrs Dowling commented to Mrs Damon that it looked rather like those old-fashioned papers of pins, and Mrs Damon replied that she could do with one of them nowadays.

'The cartridges are dummies, of course. You all know a dummy by now.' The Ladies' Shooting Class assented. They stood in a half-circle round the hearthrug while Mr Sillery and Major Puncheon explained and demonstrated.

'Do you all understand, ladies?'

'No. I don't.' Mrs Goose spoke shamelessly and seriously. When Mr Sillery renewed his explanation she listened with a critical expression, as a cat listens at a mousehole.

'Thank you. I've got it now.' She stood back a little, digesting her invisible mouse.

'Suppose the enemy don't bob up where you think they will,' said Mrs Johnson. 'Do we have to lug the whole thing round to fire it in the other direction?' A faint tinge of scorn for male impracticality was in her voice.

As Major Puncheon showed how the gun could be slewed around and raised or lowered on its stand, she smiled forgivingly. 'Very nice,' she said. 'Handy, isn't it, Mrs Cullen?'

'I seem to have heard,' said Mrs Canty, 'that machine guns get very hot. This one's water-cooled, you say. Suppose all the water gets used up, what then?'

'It would jam,' answered Major Puncheon. 'But that's been thought of. You've asked a very sensible question, Mrs Canty, but there's an answer ready for it.' He explained the cooling system.

'All the same, wouldn't it be a good plan to take a can of water along? We don't want any more trouble about running short of water, like we had last month with the fire practice.'

Mr Sillery flushed. Mrs Canty, having loosed her arrow, listened to Major Puncheon's further assurances and declared herself satisfied, for at heart, like most termagants, she was a magnanimous creature.

'I suppose it takes more strength than a rifle,' insinuated Mercy Hazard.

'Try for yourselves, ladies,' said Mr Sillery.

One by one, the twelve ladies knelt down behind the alligator, gravely, as at a shrine. Mrs Cullen, the first to experiment, pulled the bolt with such determined vehemence that she fell over backwards. No one smiled, and the others, calculating their pull as carefully as though it were some flavour going into a pudding, managed very adequately.

'Well,' said Mrs Johnson, the last to rise. 'Well, thank you very much, I'm sure. I daresay we could all manage that, at a pinch.' Which was one of the comforts, Mrs Goose was murmuring to Miss Cutler, about being a woman. One had to turn one's hand to anything, almost. One thing more or less didn't make much difference. Miss Cutler replied that, speaking for herself, she'd always had quite a liking for machinery. Once you got the hang of it, you must admit it was very reasonable. 'Though I'd be scared stiff if I had to drive a car,' she said. 'Think how you'd feel if you hurt someone accidentally.'

All this while, Mrs Ben Hazard, Mercy's sister-in-law, had not said a word. She was a long, quiet young woman, moving with a kind of uncompleted elegance, as though she were really a nymph but imperfectly educated as such. Her silence would have surprised no one, but now that it was clear that she meant to say something, the others listened, waiting for her to speak.

'Go on, Phyllis,' whispered Mercy.

'Yes, I will. Mr Sillery, Major Puncheon, there's talk going round that you ought to be told about, and I'm going to tell you. Mr de Lacy Smith has been talking about our class. And he's been saying that we'd be more use learning to milk than learning to shoot. That's what he's been saying. And you ought to know about it, I reckon.'

'Actually, I do know about it,' said Henry Sillery mildly. 'And I think we can just leave it at that.'

The class did not feel quite that way.

'*Milk!*' exclaimed Mrs Canty. 'All I can say is, I could milk Mr de Lacy Smith off his legs. And so could you, Mrs Damon, and Mrs Goose, and Mrs Cullen, and Mrs Johnson. Milk, indeed! I'd like to see him finish off our old Crumple.'

'S'pose he'll want us to learn knitting next.'

'Crochet, more likely! No one's ever got hurt with a crochet hook, I believe.'

'What I say is, why not learn milking too?' said Mrs Cullen. 'Them of us as don't know already. You come round one afternoon, Mrs Hazard, my dear. I'll soon teach you. There's a bit more knack to it than shooting, naturally, cows being what they are. But you'll soon pick it up. And that'll spike his guns – if he's got any.'

Standing by the hearth with an expression gravely demure, Mr Sillery looked uncommonly like his grandfather. Major Puncheon began dumping some wooden boxes on the table. 'Now, ladies, you must learn how to fill,' he said. 'Here are some empty belts, here is some live ammunition. The first thing to notice is . . .'

They moved towards the table, their fingers crisped, their faces mettled with emulation. Mrs Damon glanced inside an empty box.

'The picture shows you the way to put the belt back,' explained Major Puncheon.

'Very sensible, too,' approved Mrs Damon.

'This filling the belts is a job in which you ladies can be very helpful,' said Mr Sillery. 'I'm afraid it's dull. But I do assure you it's useful.'

‘And when the time comes,’ said Mrs Dowling, inserting cartridges with dexterity and thinking how like pins they were, ‘shall we sit beside our men, doing it while they shoot them off?’

‘Well, no. I’d prefer you to be doing it in a cellar. One doesn’t want to waste lives.’ Mrs Dowling worked as neatly as before, but her face fell.

‘Or ammunition,’ added Miss Cutler. ‘Suppose something came along and hit the box. It would all go off before it could be used.’ Mrs Dowling, reconciled to the cellar, agreed.

Undirected, they had settled themselves at the table before the boxes of cartridges as for a sewing party. Major Puncheon glanced at Mr Sillery, who nodded. There had been no accidents to the Ladies’ Shooting Class, but at times a certain possessiveness had shown itself, Mrs Goose in particular becoming so attached to a rifle that she had developed a long-standing insomnia (first brought on, she said, by Goose’s snores, which many a time had woken her up all of a tremble, thinking them bombs) and a conviction that a rifle handy beside the bed would be the only certain cure for it. Who knows what passions might not be aroused by an unchaperoned alligator? So the two men unshipped the machine gun and carried it away. The women worked on without comment, but a certain feeling of tension as he was leaving the room compelled Mr Sillery to remark that he hoped they would find their job more interesting now that they had seen what a machine gun looked like. There was an absence of sentiment in their farewell glances which suggested that they did not assume they had seen the last of it.

After that he had to put away the goats. Returning, he paused on the lawn and cocked his ear. Though upholding his ladies, he still could not quite believe in them, and he wanted to know what they were like when left to themselves. They were womanly enough to be talking their heads off. Presently, Mrs Cullen's voice emerged.

'When I was down in Devon helping my sister with her first baby,' she was saying, 'Bert – that's my brother-in-law – came back on compassionate leave. And he was telling us all about the Sten gun. Now, *that's* what I want to get ahold of. On the whole, it's more like a rifle, because you load it with a magazine. And in the handle there's a button marked "A", just like a telephone. When you press it one way . . .'

MUTTON'S ONLY HOUSE

c. December 1942

For the inside of a minute one could see the house from the train. Then the woods swept forward like a tongue and licked it up. They were fir woods, equally efficacious at all seasons of the year.

As a rule the people in the train were local people. If they had felt impelled to say anything about the house they would never have been so forward as to mention it before its owner. But occasionally a stranger's voice would say, 'Look! There's a house!' And now she heard a brief discussion between two soldiers as to whether or no it was a house by Lutyens. The army was like that nowadays. Upside-down like everything else.

Leaning forward, she said:

'No. It's by Mutton.'

'Mutton? Oh, I don't think I know his work. What else has he done?'

'This is Mutton's only house.'

The first soldier – they were gunners – said that was a pity, and the second said he had told him it wasn't Lutyens, not niminy-piminy enough.

Jane Mutton's pale eyes turned to the window and the pale December landscape. Her long upper lip policed any tendency to smile. Why feel gratified, why be amused? These young know-alls got on her nerves. Personally she thought Lutyens a very good architect.

It was from the train that she had first seen, ten years ago, the moderate severe sweep of hillside, the hanging fir woods. And her thoughts, occupied by considerations of a new hunter, opened to admit the query, why not build a house there? From then till the second year of the war this railway view of her house had had for her little more actuality than a minikin replica of the blueprint's *East Elevation with Stable Block*. She had known how it would look. From the moment she gave her mind to building her house she had known very clearly everything about it; but she had not given much consideration as to how it would strike the eyes of travelling strangers two miles away.

Mutton or Lutyens, it looked very well; and never better than in this wintry light, with the morning sun shining on the sharp new brick and delineating the bays and recesses of the stable block. For all that, she would rather be travelling by car.

But just as she had foreseen her house – unerringly, unassisted by architects – and, presently, there it was, looking exactly as she had intended it to look; just as all her life long she had seen how her life should develop, and duly, it was taking the shape she had decided on, Jane Mutton saw her duty in wartime, plain, indubitable, rectangular; and part of that duty was to save petrol. Local deference, the affability of local bigwigs, would have granted her all the petrol she might choose to ask for. 'My dear good Jane, of course you must have petrol. You can't fag in and out of Dunwater by puff-puff.' And implied there was the rider of 'at *your* age, my dear.' But though this was quite true, for Jane Mutton was over sixty, rectangular duty sent her off erect on a shining bicycle to catch, first the 9.50, afterwards the 8.30, to Dunwater, the county town.

Seeing everything so uncommonly clearly, Jane Mutton saw also the pitying entertainment of her friends. She would have scorned them, these soft west-country hard riders to hounds, living in houses which they had inherited, evading every wartime restriction and assuming every wartime authority to the manner born, if her wary conscience had not kept her reminded that it is unseemly to scorn people towards whom you have an obligation you would rather not recall. Evacuees. At the outbreak of war to take in evacuees had seemed the common doom, and if anyone was marked out for it, she was, living in her great new house, without even the excuse of only one inherited bathroom to plead for her. But then a Labour Councillor in Dunwater began to talk about making the rich do their share. Class loyalty closed the ranks, with one accord her friends realised how much more at home the poor evacuees would feel in cottage households; and in order to leave no gap in this philanthropic front Miss Mutton's self-made barracks was defended as zealously as though it had paid a succession of death duties.

And having seen all this quite clearly she now preferred to overlook it. As the train slowed down the two gunners began to get their traps together.

‘And that’s all till next time, children,’ remarked the plain one, and his companion, who was prettier still now that he had put on his haloing hat, made a small bow, and said:

‘En attendant le plaisir de vous revoir.’

Cook’s Tours, thought Jane Mutton instantly. In her youth, while the Mutton money was still being put together, the Mutton family group, with a solid Belfast application to what’s what, had made several Cook’s Tours, and young men like this conducted them.

For no recognisable reason she now said:

‘Are you stationed here? Would you like to see over the house, the Mutton house?’

Signalling with a large hand in a white glove she added:

‘Wait a minute, guard.’

While the train waited she told them how to get there, when to telephone, and that they must come on a Sunday. When the train moved on she found that her heart was beating like the heart of some young girl, a gay and flustered vibration.

And yet Hospitality to the Forces was one of the things that Jane Mutton did. Christmas parties. Parties to eat strawberries. Parties for convalescents from the Naval Hospital at Mugdown. Always with games, and with young girls to help with the entertaining. Her parties went off very well, like everything else she undertook. They involved a great deal of trouble, and she did them very thoroughly, and the moment they were over she began to put things straight again, folding and stacking the deckchairs, putting back the gramophone records, airing the rooms, emptying the ashtrays, collecting the crockery and carrying it to the white-tiled kitchen in which Mrs Burt, who came in daily, looked so doggedly alien to anything labour-saving.

For another of the things that Jane Mutton had seen so uncommonly clearly was that a solitary woman, however large the house she lived in, must not absorb labour in wartime. Her maids had found themselves freed in order to join the Services (they had married, however), her cook, travelling with a battery of saucepans, had been loaned to the Mugdown Hospital, her garden was made over to the Land Army, and only the stable cat remained in the stable block.

'Austerity Jane! We've all decided we simply *must* call you Austerity Jane,' shrieked Mrs Winter of Winter's Harrow; and later, on a more private shriek, remarked to her sister, Mrs Bulteel of Mugdown St Magdalen:

'It sticks out a mile. Jane Mutton *enjoys* it! She's hopelessly mean, and now she's having the time of her life cutting down expenses.'

'Trying to recoup after building that ghastly house,' said Diana Bulteel.

'When I think how Henry wore himself to the bone keeping evacuees out of it! I wish to God we'd sent the Enuretic Children there, instead of wasting ratepayers' money renting The Myrtles for them.'

For this was in 1942, when Jane Mutton had finally put herself beyond the pale of comprehension by taking a paid job on the County Administration.

'First of all she lets down the Hunt, then she lets us all down by this nonsense about not using petrol, and throwing away perfectly good servants. And now, while we're all doing voluntary work, slaving in canteens and so forth, she walks in under our very noses and pouches two quid a week as a clerk. There's only one word for it. It's *scabbing*!'

'Darling, *must* you talk like a Bolshie? All the same, scabbing's the word.'

Returning scabbily by the 5.20, Jane Mutton watched for her house. It had a way of hiding itself from south-going trains. Twice or thrice she had mislaid it thus, looked too soon or too late, thought how some casual bomb . . . there it was, a pale oblong among the darkening woods. The house by Mutton. Mutton's only house. Only Mutton's house if it came to that, for it was not admired. Cycling against the feline pressure of the west wind she thought about it, about its foundations and about its cost, about the smell of its virginity, about its particular echoes and resonances, about a chimney which had smoked and been put right, about its hidden elegancies of plumbing and lighting.

She put away the bicycle in the stable, had a word with the stable cat, and went in by the back entrance. From room to room she mounted through the house, putting up the black-outs, righting this and that, shaking a curtain to fall handsomely. In the music room (she was not musical though) she paused. It was a long, narrow room with a coffered ceiling. At one end a glass cocktail bar glittered like an up-to-date altar, an altar in the no-expense-spared style of church furnishing which reflects to the faithful how generously they have contributed. Along one wall hung her collection of modern paintings. They were without exception bright and bad: bright apples, bright acrobats, bright landscapes of blue trees or austere pink ploughland. They basked in the faultless lighting like so many suburban harlots being dined at a Mayfair restaurant.

Then she went downstairs and warmed up the supper which Mrs Burt had prepared for her, and ate it in the kitchen, where it was warm. After considering for a while she poured out a double whisky. It seemed to her she was getting a cold.

Three days to wax, three days to rage, three days to wane. The cold ran the usual course. It had gone, and she was beginning to plan for the usual Christmas party (games and young girls) when a voice on the telephone asked if we could really come over and see your house. If they wanted to see anything of it they must come early, she replied – feeling suddenly pestered and antagonistic. The voice assured her that we would.

* * *

'My cousin Hilary Mutton died in '37.'

'Indeed, miss?' Mrs Burt's tone was respectfully smitten. 'They do say that time heals old scores, but it's my belief one never appreciates a loss till it's over.'

It was Sunday morning, and Mrs Burt was helping to give things an extra rub-up. Miss Mutton switched on the Hoover, became deaf to any more condolences. Wandering, I shouldn't be surprised, thought Mrs Burt.

Jane Mutton had no doubt of it. *Mooning* was her word, supplemented by *doting* and *drivelling*. Here she was, imagining, rehearsing fancy conversations, mooning, in fact, just because two know-all young men had condescended to notice her house. That was quite enough time wasted on cleaning, she said, and Mrs Burt was dismissed, to muse on what might happen to unmarried ladies even when you might suppose them quite safely over the change.

They arrived about three o'clock, and at once in a business-like way she began to walk them round the exterior. Their comments, and the remarks exchanged between them, showed them remarkably familiar with the east front.

'Surely you didn't notice all that from the train.'

'Oh no,' said the pretty one. 'Oh Lord, no! We're on a searchlight, you see. And once or twice we've contrived to get a look at you.'

It seemed to her deeply romantic that while she lay unknowing behind the black-out their beam had probed through the darkness, nosed her out, abandoned her, and visited her again.

'Are you allowed to do that sort of thing?'

'Actually,' said the plain one, 'searchlight is pretty damaging. A house has to have composition to stand up to it. Yours does.'

While she tasted this he began to ask about Mutton. Now was the opportunity to introduce her cousin Hilary. But she did not choose to take it, walking on to where the pretty one was fondling the stable cat.

'Look, Jim, isn't she grand? A Palladian pussy!'

Jim stalked on, reached the north-east angle, paused, stepped back, paused again. A look of deep contentment flooded his face.

'There's management!' he said. Turning to her he added, 'I've been puzzling for days how Mutton disposed of that pavilion.'

'How else would you dispose of it?'

'Was he a relation of yours?' asked the pretty one conversationally. 'I often dream how marvellous it would be to have a house designed by someone who knew one, and who would put in all the things one wanted. Architects can be so intractable.'

The plain one caught her eye and grinned.

'I shouldn't exactly describe this as an obliging piece of architecture, Pinky.'

A minute later the suggestible Pinky was describing the kitchen fenestration as formidable. His plain friend then took him under control, and they stood for some ten minutes before the main façade, Jim explaining to Pinky why Mutton's pediment hit the nail on the head, while Mutton listened, rubbing her hands together, shifting from foot to foot as though in some slow dance.

'Now come and see the inside.'

Her tone of voice betrayed her. Pinky with showmanly excitement whispered:

'*It's her*. I know it!'

Then why the hell not say so? – thought the other. Mutton the architect was explicit enough, wore no dickeys. He glanced scowlingly round the entrance. He wanted to look at it, but now that confounded woman who might be Mutton would be getting between him and everything.

The stairs, whose iron balustrading gave them a sort of

rigid lightness, rose, encircling a vast newel of air, through the three storeys of the house, and finished with a circular balustrade under a shallow dome. But fully to display this she had to switch on the light, for the dome was painted over.

'Circling the square,' said Pinky.

'Octagon,' she amended.

'How you must damn the black-out,' said the plain one.

'I do.'

'Getting in the way of all your best effects.'

But she swept the attribution aside. She would accept it, but not yet, not till they had seen everything. For everything was hers.

Indeed, she was more conscious of the inside than of the outside. It had cost her more trouble. To build a house one needs only to see it, as she had seen; but colour schemes and decorations have to be looked for.

Coming indoors, the two gunners changed their rôles. It was now the pretty one who commented, admired, drew his friend's attention to this and that. Occasionally the other asserted himself with questions about some technical nicety, and in the gun room he became almost violently enthusiastic about the cupboard fittings; but for the most part he looked at the ceilings, or out of the window, or at her and out of the window again. Experience had taught that it was best to leave the music room, with refreshments, to the last. She threw open the door, switched on the faultless lighting.

'Oh, I say!' Pinky's voice had a dazzled, a dizzied note.

'*Oh my God!*'

Impossible for her, impossible for the hapless Pinky either, to brace themselves against it by resenting it as an exhibition of bad manners. It was so patently an exhibition of the heart. The words came out on a sort of remonstrating groan, sombre with disillusionment.

'How marvellous to have tea!' exclaimed Pinky, rallying his Cook's Tourists. 'Tea in a cup instead of tea in a mug!'

Immediately they began to talk about army life.

Presently everything was quite normal again, and Pinky, under his invaluable eyelashes, could steal a few glances at the modern paintings. No doubt of it, they did go too far. Poor thing! He could feel for her, for he too, according to Jim, went at times too far also. Would another slice of cake be going too far? Anyhow, he'd have it. Eating helped one over awkward patches, he had learned that in the army; and to be well lined with cake, and, oh, if possible fortified by something out of that glassy Taj Mahal, would strengthen him for the moment when he would have to say, Thank you so much for showing us over your lovely house; for to do so would now certainly fall to him.

Sad for poor James, too, bumped down to earth and now pinned there, thought Pinky fluently, by his idol's much too large feet of clay, his mutton suddenly going cold on him. He mustn't say that, though. That would be going too far. *Revenons à nos moutons.* That, too, must not be said. Watch your step, Pinky! Though sooner or later, any minute now, James, so prone to fall through his illusions, and always falling so hard, would fall out of and be through with him.

Out again in the cold, with the mist sopping the fir-woods, Pinky remarked that their hostess mixed a magnanimous cocktail. He thought he might venture that. He wanted to say something good about the woman.

'Her taste in drinks is better than her taste in decoration.'

The tone was grim, yet cheerful. For the young have great powers of self-healing; and during tea Jim re-established Mutton, an architect who knew his own mind, a fine fellow, and nothing wrong with him except the dire fatality which handed over his handsome house to be bedizened by that Jezebel; which was no fault of Mutton's.

Still on the doorstep whence she had seen them walk away, the house behind her like an empty echoing shell, she listened to their footsteps, and to the complacent *plop-plop* of the moisture falling from the boughs. It was cool and impersonal out here, and here she would stay till she had overcome the impulse to break something, anything, everything. Why all this fuss about an afternoon's fiasco? Why this idiot hankering for approval, for what people nowadays called appreciation? She had built the house to please herself, and it pleased her, and that was all there was to it, and all there need be, and all there would be. There they were, walking away, but still within earshot. Habit and army boots compelled them, already the ill-assorted pair were walking in step, walking as though they were marching. Marching away, *soldiers marching all to die*.

With the relief of a hunted fox that smells a nearby earth she remembered that the things in the music room could perfectly well wait for Mrs Burt to clear them away tomorrow morning. She was too busy. She really must get on with the arrangements for the Christmas party. With conscription for young women it was getting harder and harder to scratch up half a dozen presentable girls.

IT'S WHAT WE'RE HERE FOR

20 February 1943

Mrs Leopard slid her arms cautiously down the sleeves and wrapped the twenty-guinea coat (discard by Lady Killdew) round her alley-cat pregnancy. Lucy Bogle and Kate Larpent, Women's Voluntary Services, Crockleford, Dorsetshire, gazed at the transformation they had wrought. A minute before, Mrs Leopard's pinched face had been streaky with tears and she had sat twisting her hands in her lap. Now her face was merely pale, and her hands relaxed and fell asleep like kittens inside the fur cuffs.

Lucy Bogle turned to Kate Larpent and said warmly, 'It fits her beautifully, doesn't it?'

'It needs shortening,' said Kate Larpent. 'Are you good at sewing, Mrs Leopard?'

Mrs Leopard replied that she could do anything with a needle.

'A good wrap-over too,' added Lucy Bogle. 'Now forget all your troubles and go off and have a nice lunch at the British Restaurant. We've got a wonderful British Restaurant. And remember, there's nothing more for you to worry about.

Lodgings, milk, clinic – we'll get everything fixed for you. That's what we're here for.' Mrs Leopard crossed the office, past empty jam pots and heaps of clothing and mounds of soldiers' socks. Kate Larpent looked after her.

'One moment,' she called. 'What about shoes? You mustn't go about with your heels all worn down. You might trip.'

Mrs Leopard obediently sat down and removed a battered pump. 'Threes,' she said.

Murmuring something about those land girl shoes, so nice and solid, Lucy Bogle buried herself in a closet. Mrs Leopard took off a white cotton sock, rolled down a silk stocking, exposed an ankle. Kate Larpent turned slightly green and said in a controlled voice, 'That's bad.'

'Awful!' Mrs Leopard agreed. 'Oh, they're awful. Sometimes I don't hardly know how to walk. That's why I gave up that job at the hospital. Those stone floors. I couldn't stand it, really.'

Emerging from the closet, Lucy Bogle dropped a pair of shoes with a crash which proclaimed their solidity.

'Good heavens!' she exclaimed. 'Your *poor* veins! You must go to the clinic this very afternoon.'

Mrs Leopard pulled up her stocking, put on the sock, glanced briefly at the land girl shoes, and replaced her pump.

'I'll ring up the doctor right away,' Lucy Bogle said. 'We've got a wonderful clinic.'

Mrs Leopard began to cry again. 'I was going to see the children this afternoon,' she said. 'I'd got a woolly for David and a little dress for Jean, and some chocolates off my ration.'

'But there's no bus to Long Twizzel today. And you can't possibly walk,' Lucy Bogle said.

Mrs Leopard wept more bitterly. 'I worry about them so.'

'Of *course* you do,' said Lucy Bogle. 'But you needn't. You said yourself how well they looked when you saw them last week, and how much they'd grown since they've been there.'

'They're well enough,' Mrs Leopard said, 'but their clothes are awful. And so dirty, too. They look like country children.' Her voice faded in despair.

'I daresay they're a little grubby,' Lucy Bogle said. 'But think how happy they are with Mrs Welland. Even if she *is* rather a slattern, she's got a heart of gold.'

'Ever since they was evacuated,' said Mrs Leopard, 'Mrs Welland has been writing to say they needed this and that. Every week I've sent her money. Twenty-five shillings, and thirty shillings. Sent registered. I've stinted myself to send money to her. And she's had all my coupons, too. And when I went there, they were in rags.'

'We'll soon put that right,' said Lucy Bogle. 'That's what we're here for. This afternoon Mrs Larpent will try to find some nice, warm clothes for them – let me see, David's five and Jean's seven – and then you can take them out by the Saturday bus. The clinic will have given you your first injection by then, and you'll be feeling so much stronger.'

'I don't want to say anything against Mrs Welland. I daresay she's kind at heart,' Mrs Leopard continued. 'But I couldn't help speaking a bit sharp to her when I saw the state they were in. She didn't like it. I could see that. And now I'm afraid she's taking it out on the children.'

'Oh no!' Lucy Bogle cried. 'She's the kindest, most motherly woman!'

'They aren't her children,' said Mrs Leopard. Her grief had communicated itself to the coat. It looked a second-hand coat now, shabby and downtrodden.

After Mrs Leopard had gone reluctantly off to the clinic, Lucy Bogle said to the silently tidying Kate Larpent, 'Say what you will, Kate, it's the child that matters.'

Together they reread the investigator's note containing Mrs Leopard's brief and lamentable history:

> Confidential. Mrs Leopard, Londoner. Mother of two evacuated children at Mrs Welland, Long Twizzel. Husband in the army, serving in Middle East. Pregnant. Baby due in December. Husband left England in February. Now lodging at 3 Vine Terrace, but landlady will not keep her after Sept. 19th. Receives army allowance but bad manager. Not wholly desirable character.

'How many children has Mrs Welland – children of her own?' asked Kate Larpent.

'Six, I think, or seven. Why? That wouldn't make any difference. She's a born mother.'

'I daresay Mrs Leopard's coupons would make a considerable difference,' said Kate Larpent, and tore up the note.

'Oh, Kate, what a wonderful *rock* you are! You always look at things in such an unprejudiced way!' Lucy Bogle exclaimed gratefully.

For two ladies looking at things in an unprejudiced way, Lucy Bogle and Kate Larpent got a good deal of emotional release out of managing everything for Mrs Leopard. A pair of shoes, size three and practically new, was obtained from Lady Killdew, the only member of the local W.V.S. whose feet were not sensibly broad and untrammelled. Old Miss Ensor, so kind and so clean, was persuaded to make over her parlour as a bed-sitting room, and the billeting authorities were persuaded to pay part of the rent. On the plea that flannelette was impossible for a winter baby, the standard layette was considerably embellished. On the hypothesis that morality is entirely a matter of self-respect, the storeroom was combed for undergarments which would help Mrs Leopard to think well of herself. Lucy Bogle, replying to the torn-up note, assured the investigator that the WVS would gladly cope with Mrs Leopard. It was what they were there for, rather than to judge anyone's private life. Kate Larpent, in the course of a telephone conversation with Mrs Dimple, WVS representative at Long Twizzel, lured Mrs Dimple into some parochial reflections on painted London mothers coming down and unsettling evacuees and then bit her head off with the reply that painted London mothers were more hygienic than dirty country ones. And the report of the clinic doctor that Mrs Leopard weighed ninety-four pounds, had five bad teeth, and needed special care was hailed by Lucy Bogle and Kate Larpent as a personal triumph.

Miss Ensor's bed-sitting room, Lady Killdew's shoes, and the morally stimulating underclothes, however, had to wait for more than a week before Mrs Leopard reappeared. She had been to London, she explained, to see her mother. She looked more ill – and more dramatically fragile – than ever. It was distressing that on the heels of this quite plausible explanation Mrs Dimple should visit the office to report that for the last week Mrs Leopard had been frequenting the Rose and Crown at Long Twizzel and drinking sherry all day with a young civilian who had a dark complexion, wore pointed shoes, and left without paying the bill.

'I can only hope he is the father of the child,' she said.

Kate Larpent replied in her most unprejudiced tones, 'I have always understood that the father of a child born in wedlock is the child's father.'

Mrs Leopard, returned from London, as she explained, was pleased with the shoes and glad to hear of Miss Ensor's bed-sitting room. But the underclothes brought tears to her eyes. 'They're lovely, I'm sure. I bought a rayon dress for my Jean, just this colour, and sent it down for her birthday. But when I asked Mrs Welland where it was, she said it never got there. You're so kind, you WVS ladies, I don't suppose you'd think evil of anyone. But why are my David and my Jean in rags and the little Wellands all dressed up to the nines? If I could have a little place of my own, and all of us be together, I wouldn't worry so. But all my things, except a few forks, went in the blitz.'

'You mustn't worry now,' Lucy Bogle said to her. 'David and Jean have all the clothes they need. We made up a specially good parcel and Mrs Dimple took it to Mrs Welland herself.'

'I didn't see any new clothes,' Mrs Leopard said. 'I went up every day but one last week, but that Mrs Welland, she never said a word about new clothes, and both the children looked like something the cat brought in.' Persuaded to accept Miss Ensor's bed-sitting room in lieu of a little place all her own, Mrs Leopard departed, clutching a hot-water bottle.

'Poor thing, how very incompetently she lies,' said Kate Larpent. 'One can't help feeling sorry for her.'

Lucy Bogle agreed. It was so hard on the baby that was coming, she added. And it was the baby, wasn't it, that they were concentrating on?

During the next week the life that was coming called for no attentions, but on the morning of October 6th Kate Larpent looked up from a sea of socks and observed that they might expect Mrs Leopard at any moment.

'Oh! Oh, dear! Poor creature. Do you really expect her?' Lucy Bogle asked.

'On a cycle.'

'But, good heavens, Kate, she mustn't bicycle. It would be –'

Just then Lady Killdew came in with several recipes for green-tomato chutney collected in India. Most of the spices, as she observed, would have to be cut out, and one couldn't expect to find tamarinds, mangosteens, and okra in Dorset. But she didn't suppose anybody would know the difference if the WVS fell back on apples. 'And by the way,' she added, 'talking of apples and the autumn, do you think your poor little Mrs What's-Her-Name could be persuaded to use a rather quieter pub? It distresses my husband to see me so constantly vanishing into the snug of the Pure Drop, especially as he paid for that coat.'

Lady Killdew was followed by Miss Ensor, who was very sorry, but would Mrs Bogle find other lodgings for Mrs Leopard, please? She would rather not say more, since every one of those Commandos was some mother's son and ready to die at any moment, God bless them.

When Mrs Leopard came in, the subject of lodgings was troubling her also. The idea of a little place of her own, where she could have the children, and the forks, and a few little extras to make out with, had quite taken hold of her, she said. Sorry as she was to disappoint that dear old Miss Ensor, she didn't feel she could settle anywhere but in a little place of her own. 'Speaking for myself, I'd put up with anything,' she said. 'You know what I'm like, you know I'm not one to ask for things. But it's my David and my Jean. I can't leave them there to be trampled on day and night. Their father worships those children, and if he knew the way that Mrs Welland – '

The telephone rang and Kate Larpent answered it. It was Mrs Dimple, who wished to report that she had taken those clothes up to the little Leopards and did the WVS know that the police had come to Mrs Welland's cottage about some woollen vests which Mrs Leopard had sent? . . . No? Well, they had. Mrs Welland had put the vests on the children only that morning, and when the police saw them, they said they were the ones the store had reported stolen and had taken them away there and then. Wasn't it dreadful?

'I'll enquire into it at once,' said Kate Larpent briskly. 'Of course it's atrocious. And quite unlawful. I suppose it was your local policeman? Thank you so much for reporting it.' She replaced the receiver as though she were putting a sword back into the scabbard. Inside the warm coat Mrs Leopard was trembling convulsively. Her mouth hung open and her black eyes rolled like fruit that the wind will in a moment smite off the bough.

'I think I'll go off now and have a look for a little place.' She rose, and then uttered a cry of anguish and sat down again, clasping her belly.

Tea, a hot-water bottle, smelling salts from Lucy Bogle, a cigarette from Kate Larpent, sal volatile from the chemist's, and the gas fire turned on regardless of fuel restrictions presently turned Mrs Leopard to a delicate pink and got her mouth shut. Lucy Bogle rang up her doctor, who gave it as his opinion that Mrs Leopard was clearly a case for the infirmary. But of course they must get her consent to it.

Both ladies were remarkably eloquent and persuasive about the beauties of the infirmary.

'It's nothing to be ashamed of, you know,' Kate Larpent said. 'All you'll want is a nice dressing gown, and *we'll* see to that. We've got such a specially nice infirmary here, not like an infirmary at all. And you'll have company, you know. No more lonely nights, no more trudging from shop to shop on those poor feet of yours.'

'They'll let you smoke, you know,' said Lucy Bogle.

'You'll be *so* happy there,' Kate Larpent continued. 'You'll be so comfortable you'll never want to come out.'

'Of course you can come out when you like,' Mrs Bogle assured her.

'*We* shall look after the children,' Kate Larpent said. 'I shall go over to Long Twizzel tomorrow. Myself.'

Mrs Leopard sat up, blazing. 'Don't you believe a word she says! I swear to you by the living God, Mrs Bogle, that there Mrs Welland is the awfullest liar that ever went about behind an apron.'

She finished off a cup of cold tea and promised to come back after lunch, when the WVS would have arranged everything and the Relieving Officer would be there to meet her. Everything was arranged with guilty alacrity. Kate Larpent observed once or twice how admirable the Public Services were. Lucy Bogle said how it would have delighted Charles Dickens.

'By the way, Kate,' she asked, 'who was it that rang up while she was here? Wasn't there something about a policeman?'

'Policeman?' Kate Larpent appeared to be searching her memory. The telephone rang. She snatched off the receiver and handed it to Lucy Bogle. Lady Killdew became audible.

'Is that you, Lucy? I've got a message for you from your Mrs What-You-Call-Her. I recognised her – at least I recognised my coat – and I asked how she was. She asked me to tell you that she had found lodgings after all. She had met a friend and was going back with her by bus. To stay indefinitely.'

'Yes,' said Lucy Bogle. 'How – how nice. How excellent. Did she say who the friend was?'

'Oh yes. She introduced me. A hearty, round-about sort of person. But of course you know her. She's the foster mother to Mrs Panther's evacuee children. Why are you laughing, Lucy? Isn't she Panther?'

'No, dear – Leopard. Did she say anything else?'

'No, nothing in particular. Just the usual things. How she wouldn't know where she was without the WVS. And so on.'

ENGLISH CLIMATE

1 May 1943

As Gunner Brock opened the door of the recreation hut a volley of rain came in, and a cat. He shut the door and turned to look at the cat. It was a new ginger, he noted. Cats came and went on the anti-aircraft site, and this annoyed Gunner Brock, who had a tidy mind and felt that cats should be permanent. One grievance flicked him into voicing another. 'Perhaps you'll have got those books changed by the time I'm back,' he said to Gunner Ives who was sunk deep in a chair, reading.

A dozen exhausted volumes sagged on a shelf by the door. Their subject matter did not so much express the eclecticism of the Welfare Officer who had brought them out from the library a fortnight earlier as the fact that he had chosen them after lunching protractedly with a friend.

'Not till I've finished *The Wide Wide World,*' said Gunner Ives, who was a Marxist. 'Just listen to this. . . .'

Gunner Brock fidgeted with one foot and then the other and finally interrupted him. 'I've got to catch my train,' he said.

‘Well,’ Gunner Ives said, his glance still drawn irresistibly towards the paragraph he had been reading. ‘So long. Have a good leave.’

‘Thanks,’ Brock said, and went out into the rain.

It was a five-mile walk to the station, and the last mile and a half he hurried, but he needn’t have done so; the afternoon train was nearly twenty minutes late. He found a seat, and began his journey of nineteen hours and five changes. The railway track ran within half a mile of the anti-aircraft site. Through the streaming window he saw briefly the huts, the smoke from the cookhouse chimney, the searchlight and the locator in their canvas hoods. It looked as though some demented fair had set itself up on the heath and now waited for the arrival of customers.

By midday tomorrow he would be home. At midday tomorrow it would still be raining. He would spend the afternoon having a bath, wallowing at full length, hearing the chirp of rain in the gutters and the gentle wallop of the bath-water running down the overflow pipe. There he would lie, reading. And downstairs would be Mother, rattling the tea things, Edna coming home from her office, then Dad. At seven Mother and Edna would go off to the YMCA canteen, splashing so bravely through the wet. How on earth did women support life when there wasn’t a war? What would Mother do when this war was over and the canteen was closed and she was left with but one son (if that, indeed) instead of those dozens of ‘my boys’, towards all of whom she felt like a mother? A retired colonel, however fire-eating, takes up gardening or plays golf or bridge or busies himself with local administration or rings migratory birds, for men are flippant, variable, easily amused. But to a woman's iron energies what appeasement can peace bring?

Left to themselves he and Dad would wash up and get supper. The cat, the fixed and proper family cat, would rub round their legs. Once again he would feel that profound sensation of being indoors – a far more intimate sensation than that of merely being at home. Gradually he would adjust himself to small rooms, unechoing floors, passages, stairways, the complexity of a house. And upstairs his bedroom, close-fitting as a thimble, would wait for him: silently, privately, intensely, it would await the moment when he switched on the bedside lamp and shut the door after him. In that room he would slowly and luxuriously undress and luxuriously slide between the sheets and find the hot-water bottle, and lie for a breathing space listening to the rain, summoning his senses for that journey of the hand to the bookshelf. Which should it be? The fourth from the left was *Boswell's Life*, then the even ranks of the *Fitzgerald Letters*. In his fingers stirred a consciousness of how that bookshelf would feel: the orderly row, the smooth backs, the sharp corners – a world away from that heap of flaccid derelicts by the door of the recreation hut.

Waking at a burst of light and cold morning air as three schoolboys, smelling freshly of soap and early rising, climbed in over his legs, Gunner Brock saw that the weather had cleared. The sun was rising into a sky full of wind and movement. Presently he changed into the last of his trains. It was a stopping train, and the last two hours of his journey enforced the sense of homecoming, for the new passengers had the familiar local accent and intonation and talked of people and of places that he knew. At the stop before Dumbridge a woman got in who said: 'Why, I do believe it's young Mr Brock, isn't it?' and told him how wonderful his mother was, doing so much yet always ready to take on more, and Edna was wonderful too, the woman added. All this was dulling to the edge of arrival. He seemed to have been arriving for hours. As he walked down the Station Road towards the High Street, home seemed to him primarily a place where he could put down his traps.

Turning into the High Street, he experienced a momentary impression that there had been an air raid. Heaped on the pavements were bedsteads and fire-irons and kettles; Boy Scouts and Girl Guides were pushing handcarts laden with bundles of clothes; on the wine-merchant's doorstep was a parcel of parchment-bound ledgers neatly fastened together, and from the house beyond an old woman came out who carried a bird cage and a large tolling handbell. The Union Jack flew from the church tower. Stretched across the street, banging and bellying in the wind, was a wide calico streamer: DUMB . . . NATION . . . AGE. . . 'DUMBRIDGE NATIONAL SALVAGE WEEK.' Midway up the street was a whippet tank, so flimsy, so outmoded, that for an instant he supposed that some citizen cherishing it as a garden ornament had now relinquished it for salvage, but of course it was there to show the good people of Dumbridge what could be done with their iron bedsteads. Beyond the whippet tank was a long meandering trail, a dingy caterpillar whose meaning became clear to him as a woman's voice behind exclaimed: 'Just look at the book mile! Where on earth have they all come from?''What a clearance!' replied her companion.

At first he thought he would turn into a side street and so avoid this *auto-da-fé* of disgraced books laid out ready for the junk collectors. But he was too angry to spare himself, and walked on, countering his distress by reflecting on the kind of books Dumbridge could muster up: *The Scarlet Pimpernel, Hints to Fly Fishers, Anecdotes of European Courts*, and volumes of poetry called *Tally-Ho* or *By Quiet Waters*. 'If I see a copy of *Jessica's First Prayer*, I'll pinch it for Ives,' he told himself.

So inevitably he began to look, to loiter. *Montaigne's Essays* – good Lord, who would have thought Dumbridge could produce them! *Paradise Lost* – that was not so surprising. *Letters of Queen Victoria* – oh, poor Ives! *The Collected Poems of Edward Thomas* – now who, he wondered, owning that and reading it too, for it had the unmistakable warmed look of a well-read copy, could have cast it out into a book mile? He picked it up. The moment it was in his hand, as though some electricity leaped from the book to the man, he knew whose copy it was. He did not need the confirmation of the flyleaf: *Edwin Brock. April, 1934*. He put it back and walked on, as though walking on would annul what had happened. But the book mile kept up with him; in a moment he would be compelled to open his senses again, to walk slowly, to trail his glance from cover to cover, waiting for another recognition. What tomfoolery! He would go back and rescue it. It was his book.

A voice said: 'Edwin Brock, I do declare!' It was Mr Cheeseman, chemist and town councillor of Dumbridge and an old family friend. 'Delighted to see you, my boy! I thought it must be you from the way you were studying those old books. You were always one for books, weren't you? Well, what do you think of it? Pretty good, eh?'

'Is there really a mile of it?'

'Well, between you and me, no. But it goes as far as the Boer Memorial. And every inch of it a gift, you know.'

'People bring their books, do they?' Edwin asked. 'And add them on?'

'Some do,' Mr Cheeseman said. 'On our opening day you should have seen them come running out of their houses. Of course, by now it's beginning to dry up and we have to help out the look of it by books that have come in as ordinary salvage. But it's all genuine salvage, genuine Dumbridge Borough salvage, whoever puts it there. As for the old garden hoses and the brass door-knobs and the aluminium, you'd never believe it. Why, people have even brought out their medals!'

My *Fitzgerald's Letters* must be here somewhere, Brock thought; the old *Bevis* I bought when I was thirteen, and dropped into the river, and dived for; and my Nonesuch *Swift*.

'And every scrap of it good for something,' said Mr Cheeseman with reverence. 'Every scrap of it useful at long last. You can tell the Army that we're doing our best for you. Well, here we are at the Memorial. And you can see it comes right up to here. I'm going your way, as it happens, so I'll walk with you. Mill Street looks a bit naked, doesn't it, with the railings gone?'

'Yes, it does a bit.'

'There's your mother waiting for you,' Mr Cheeseman said.

She was standing on the doorstep, some knitting in her hands. When she saw Edwin, she waved the knitting and then added some more stitches.

'Here's my boy!'

Her first glance was for his sleeve. No stripes – and as he had foreseen, her face fell. Then, just as he had also foreseen, she reassumed that air of resolute buoyancy, the expression which in old days he and Edna had called Mother's Mrs Greatheart, and began to tell him how well he looked, how much broader he had grown, and that she had actually got a duck for dinner, though of course it was only a small one.

'I explained to Mr Hawes that you were coming back on leave,' she said, 'and he swore to do his utmost. People are so wonderfully kind! Oh, and that reminds me, Mr Cheeseman, I can't manage Thursday, because I am at Report Centre in the morning, and then I shall be packing Prisoners' Parcels instead of poor Mrs West – it's so sad for her that she gets these incessant colds just now – and after that I have the canteen, of course, and then the Working Party, and then the canteen again. Besides, I must keep a morsel of time for my Edwin now he's here.'

She laid her hand on his disgraceful sleeve and continued to discuss dates with Mr Cheeseman. Edna appeared. She looked extraordinarily tired, shabby, and sterile. 'So you managed to get off for the duck and Edwin,' said her mother.

Indoors, there was a delicious smell of roast duck and a smell of daffodils. The table was spread with a damask so white that it seemed to sparkle, and by his place was his old mug and two bottles of beer. Edna went to wash her hands.

'My darling!' Mrs Brock said to her son. 'My ducky! How I've been longing for this!' And for that moment she was quite genuine, and looked old and careworn and at the same time girlishly excited and vulnerable.

'Edna looks rotten,' he said. 'What's wrong with her?'

Instantly his mother began to bridle.

'I daresay she's tired. We're all a little tired, you know. And then, poor Edna, it's rather depressing for her not being allowed to join up in the ATS. But Mr Ransom won't release her. And as I tell her, even if she has to stay in a civilian job, she's freeing someone else, so really it's just the same thing.'

'Better money, anyway.'

All through the meal it was like that. A devil spoke, not he, snubbing every advance, deriding every brag. And the poor old woman, gallant and obtuse, came back every time for more punishment. Even the duck he could only praise by saying that one didn't get that sort of food in canteens, and a mention of fire-watching provoked a belittling enquiry as to how many bombs had fallen on Dumbridge – none, as he well knew, having fallen. Yet he had not meant it, and even now did not mean it. Walking beside old Cheeseman, he had settled with himself that it was no use scolding over spilt milk, that there was nothing for it but philosophy. One was always being philosophic in the army, so why not be philosophic at home too, where at least there was peace and quiet to be won by keeping one's temper? But suddenly there was nothing left but to know the worst, and pushing back his chair he ran from the room.

When he came back Edna was carrying out a trayful of dishes. His mother was sitting by the window. Her knitting was on her lap, but for once she was not knitting. She was looking at a pot of newly opened daffodils and blinking, as though their pure colour hurt her eyes.

'What's happened to my books?' he cried. 'What have you been doing with my books?'

She turned to him, and it intensified his fury to see that her expression was one of relief. 'Your books, darling? I brought them down here, to keep dry. All the good ones – your prizes and the encyclopaedia.'

'Oh!' he said. 'Then why did I see so many of them in that damned book mile of yours?'

'Oh, those were only the old things. Edna and I went through them most carefully, I'm sure. And one must do something,' she added, losing her temper because she was afraid; 'we poor civilians in a poor old town that doesn't even get a bomb on it. Surely you wouldn't grudge a few old books for national salvage! Think what it means to the country!'

'Why didn't you burn them,' he said, 'and get some fun out of it, like they do in Germany?'

'Burn them? *Burn a book?* Why, for months now we've been lighting the fires with gorse and shavings. There's no paper burned in this house, I can tell you. Every scrap of it goes into salvage. Burn a book? Why, your father's even given up his shaving calendar!'

Edwin began to laugh. He laughed on and on, like a machine, for each idiot peal deferred the moment when he would have to decide between keeping his grudge or going to retrieve what he could from the book mile.

His mother went to the door. 'Edna!' she called. 'Edna, take your mac. It's coming on to rain again, a regular downpour. Such a pity, on Edwin's first afternoon, too!' And returning she knelt down stiffly before the grate, saying that on such a wretched afternoon they really must have a fire.

BOW TO THE RISING SUN

12 June 1943

'Some girls,' said Miss Doris Butt, assistant to Mr Caldecott, of the Fuel Control Office, 'would get married right away and start a baby. Not that I should find it so difficult, but I'm not the sort of girl that would. I shouldn't feel it right, somehow. Would you, Mrs Stanley?'

The older woman murmured that she wouldn't, and went on searching through the file labelled *Memos from Ministry*.

'Though, of course, it wouldn't apply to you, would it?' Miss Butt said.

Again the older woman murmured her agreement. At 9 a.m. she had become a clerk. It was now noon, and it seemed to her that during the last three hours she had gained considerable insight into Miss Butt's private life but regrettably little into the running of the Fuel Control Office.

'No, of course not,' Miss Butt said. 'For one thing, you're married already, and for another, you're over the age. Can't you find it?'

'It doesn't seem to be here,' Mrs Stanley said.

'Never mind. Maybe it isn't. Maybe I put it into *Pending*.

Dear, dear, I'm afraid you'll be rather lost without me! But you won't be the only one. Poor Mr Caldecott, he'll be quite a lost soul, really. You see, he depends so much. Of course, it isn't as though I were going into the ATS. When Mr Caldecott called me in and told me that, try as he would, he really couldn't get me deferred again, he said to me, "Now, on no account, Miss Butt, are you to worry. I'll see you don't get sent into the ATS." And I said to him, "No, indeed, Mr Caldecott. I'm sure you couldn't bear to think of my legs in khaki stockings." Of course, you see, having worked for him so long, I can say that sort of thing to him. It cheers him up, I daresay. I expect he'll miss me. I'm always so bright, you see. A smile for everything and everyone. Besides, I understand him. Still, it's got to be. My King and Country want me. That's what they said in the last war, isn't it?'

'Yes,' said Mrs Stanley.

'Those last-war songs are having quite a comeback, aren't they? They're a bit hymny, but swinging them puts more life into them, doesn't it? I can't abide anything without life in it. I suppose you can remember the last war quite well? And I wasn't even born then. Somehow, it seems funny, doesn't it?'

'Is this it?' Mrs Stanley asked, handing her a mimeographed sheet.

'Yes, that's it. That's what you've got to go by now. So you'd better cast your eye over it.'

Mrs Stanley began to read. Miss Butt began to sing. Her voice had an appealing youthful roughness. Like the fubsy down on young bracken shoots, thought Mrs Stanley, trying to concentrate on Kitchen Nuts and Bath and Bristol Coke.

'Then there's anthracite,' Miss Butt said. 'Anthracite's tricky.'

'Why?' Mrs Stanley asked.

'Well, you see, it's mostly the better people who want it, people with furnaces, and they generally leave it to the last moment and then come in about it. I've got a list of them somewhere, but I expect I've mislaid it. You see, I know them so well. There's Miss Stebbins and the Reverend Cash and Miss Rylands – oh, she's a nuisance, that Miss Rylands! Comes in covered with shopping and says, "Where's the Fuel Controller? I want to see him personally." And poor Mr Caldecott, he absolutely dreads the sight of her, and I have to invent no end of excuses. Mrs Grandison – she's nice, she is; old Colonel Prowse, Viscount Abington, Mr Hume-Pinney. Oh dear, what a shock it will be to them when they come in expecting to see me and find you! Lots of them bring me flowers. They know I'm so passionately devoted to flowers. But Mrs Grandison generally brings eggs. Well, I suppose you've read all that by now. Now you might as well enter these up. It'll all help to give you an idea of the hang of things.' Miss Butt leaned back and began to polish her nails.

'Knowing how to manage them,' she said presently, 'that's the important thing. It just makes all the difference. The day I was called for my interview I heard Mr Caldecott ringing up the Labour Exchange. "You ought to send Miss Butt into the Diplomatic Service," he said. "She's got the human touch." Of course, I do think he exaggerates. I'm not so marvellous as he makes out. I just don't bite their heads off the way he does. Still, you've got to have the human touch, though personally

I've always found people perfectly sweet, especially the better sort of people, you understand. They come in raging, but somehow I soothe them down and they go away all smiles. There's Mr Hume-Pinney, for instance. Well, last month he came in and he said to me, "Button" – lots of them call me Button; sort of short for Butt, and me being so tiny, it's natural – "Button," he said, "why have you sent me coke? I thought you loved me." "Why, yes," I said. "Wasn't there a message pinned to that coke – *With Love from Doris*?" And believe it or not, he went off perfectly happy, and it never even came out that Mrs Grandison really had got his coal. Actually, you see, I'd got their applications mixed up. I suppose that's what Mr Caldecott means by the human touch. And that's what you'll have to concentrate on, Mrs Stanley, if you want any peace in this job. Otherwise it's squabble, squabble, squabble the whole time. Of course, I do admit it's a bit of a strain, always being a little ray of sunshine, but – You can take that call.'

A moment later Miss Butt snatched the receiver out of Mrs Stanley's hand. 'Good *morning*, Colonel Prowse. . . . Yes, it's me. It's Miss Butt speaking. . . . What? . . . Oh dear! Your greenhouses again? You know, what you need is a coal mine all of your own, really it is. Of course, we can't promise anything absolutely, but . . . Yes! That would be best. You come in and explain it all.'

Putting back the receiver, Miss Butt flew to the window sill, removed some rather exhausted daffodils to the wastepaper basket, and emptied their vase out of the window. Then she straightened her table a little and flicked some dust off the filing cabinet. Glancing at Mrs Stanley, she seemed for a moment to contemplate freshening up the older woman's appearance too. Instead she sat down and began to renovate her make-up, busy as a kitten cleaning itself, and for five minutes was perfectly silent.

Then, with newly reddened lips, she began talking once more. 'Now, Colonel Prowse, who'll be coming in presently, is just what I've been saying. In fact, Mr Caldecott says straight out he's one of my conquests. Personally, I think he's rather an old dear. But you've got to take him the right way, you know, and be sympathetic about his old greenhouses and not mind his jokes, which are a bit Anglo-Indian, I admit.'

Mrs Stanley put a sheet in her typewriter and began to type. Miss Butt raised her voice. 'Copying that memo now? You are taking hold, aren't you? Of course, I daresay when you're here it will all get more official. Everyone thinks I look such a baby, and I expect that's one reason why people like Colonel Prowse tend to make rather a pet of me and think me so marvellously efficient. Not that I'm anything out of the way, I'm sure. I'm just nice to them, and of course I never forget a face, and I've got a sense of humour. That's my little secret, really. How to win friends and influence people. Do you know, there was a book in America called *How to Win* –'

The door opened. Miss Butt sprang up, radiant and condescending. 'Good morning, Colonel Prowse.'

'Good morning, Miss Butt.'

Looking up from her typing, Mrs Stanley wondered why he had been referred to as old Colonel Prowse. Erect and trim, he had an appearance of indomitable middle age, and he carried a large bunch of pink carnations with almost completely successful assurance.

Miss Butt's glance slanted over the bouquet. Still holding it, he said: 'It's about my greenhouses, Miss Butt. I've just made over another of them for tomatoes and I must have extra heat. I've got a Land Girl, I've got some fertiliser, and now all I need is a little heat. Eh? Do you see my point, Miss Butt? Of course you do. You see everything, clever little girl that you are. So now, what about it?'

'Well, Colonel Prowse, I'll certainly mention it to Mr Caldecott when he comes in this afternoon. After all these preparations you do deserve a little encouragement, don't you?'

'I'll say I do.' Colonel Prowse nodded. His glance flickered over towards Mrs Stanley, an examining, questioning, disparaging glance.

'Colonel Prowse, I've got something to break to you,' Miss Butt said. 'Something terrible!'

'Eh? What's that?'

'You're losing me, Colonel Prowse. You're going to lose your Button. I've been called up.'

'Good Lord!'

'Yes, they can't do without me any longer. Things must be pretty desperate, mustn't they, if they can't do without poor little me?'

'Rotten,' Colonel Prowse said. He was now studying Mrs Stanley more attentively.

'Never mind, Colonel Prowse,' Miss Butt said. 'You're

going to have Mrs Stanley instead. And I've just been telling her she must be specially kind to you.'

Still holding his flowers, Colonel Prowse moved across the room. 'How do you do, Mrs Stanley? I hope Miss Butt hasn't been prejudicing you against me. I try not to be more of a nuisance than I can help.'

'Yes, I've been putting her wise about you. The gypsy's warning, you know.'

Now he was standing by the typewriter. 'Well, Mrs Stanley,' he said, 'I hope you won't find it too bad here. You know, I think it's pretty marvellous the way people like you take on these awful jobs. I can see you know all about typing, though. That's a lovely bit of work you've got in there. It's a pity you shouldn't have a nicer office. It ought to be done up.'

'Well, Colonel Prowse, and what about beginning with my poor empty flower vase?' Miss Butt said.

'Eh? Oh yes! Flowers,' Colonel Prowse said. 'Yes, I generally try to bring a few flowers along to sort of brighten things up. These are nothing much, I'm afraid. But I've got some tulips coming on, and then there'll be roses. I'm rather proud of my roses.'

He laid down his bouquet by the typewriter and said: 'Well, I mustn't keep you ladies from your lunch. So it's goodbye, is it, Miss Butt? Best of luck, and thanks for all you've done for me. You'll remember about my little business, won't you, and put it through with Caldecott? Or perhaps I should ask Mrs Stanley to see about it?'

After the door had closed and the brisk footsteps died away, Miss Butt said: 'Don't you think he's rather sweet? So touching, the way he brings his flowers along and then gets all shy about them and dumps them down anywhere. Well, thank God it's lunchtime! We'll go to the Old World, shall we? Want to wash your hands? You go first.'

In the cloakroom Mrs Stanley found herself crying, weeping unavailing tears for the desperate idiot valour of the young.

SWEETHEARTS AND WIVES

4 December 1943

Sometimes Justina and Midge discussed what would happen if all their husbands came on leave together. Lettice could go to her grandmother's – but then William would not see her, and really she was now a nice, displayable baby. The Sheridans might find a double bed at the farm – but that would not take away Roy and the twins, and if Mrs Sheridan slept out, one could not expect her to be back in time to get breakfast. Justina and Tom might have a little honeymoon at The Griffin – but that, as Midge said, would break up the household.

Without husbands the household consisted of three women and four children. Justina, who liked figures, had worked out that the average age of the party was thirteen. If one left out Mrs Sheridan, who was over thirty, the average age fell to eight years and nine months; but to leave out Mrs Sheridan except arithmetically was inconceivable, for Mrs Sheridan was the kingpin and glory of the establishment: she cooked.

Both Justina and Midge had married early in 1940. To their respective mothers it seemed natural, since both husbands were in the Forces, that they should stay on at home, keeping their spirits up, poor little things, by giving a helping hand in country houses suddenly denuded of servants and enlarged by such creative activities as organising First Aid Points, entertaining Polish officers, and breeding table rabbits. When they decided to set up house together in Badger Cottage, it seemed hopefully probable that the poor darlings would soon tire of cooking for themselves – the more so as Badger Cottage was such a disadvantageous dwelling, lonely, ugly, derelict, miles from any shop, and all the water needing to be pumped by hand. But the discovery of Mrs Sheridan quenched this hope. Mrs Sheridan was also married to a fighting man; he had been a circus hand, now he was in the RASC. Mrs Sheridan, bombed out of Mitcham, had come to Suffolk to find a home for herself, her three children, her Alsatian dog, and her horse. The horse had associations. Mrs Sheridan could not bear to be parted from it. The billeting officer had washed his hands of her when a fight between the Alsatian and Justina's two poodles elicited the fact that Mrs Sheridan would do anything and everything for whoever made a kind home for her and her beautiful Shirley. Midge's baby immunised her from conscription, but the poodles could not do the same for Justina, who had been directed to replace an auctioneer's clerk in the local town. By privily dismembering her bicycle, hiding its fragments in a fox covert, and declaring it as stolen, she was in a position to claim Shirley as an essential means of transport. The horse thereby received a ration, Mrs Sheridan was able to live with them and be their cook, and when the Alsatian was reconciled to the poodles the compound household worked perfectly.

Another of Mrs Sheridan's beauties was her farmer friend, Mr Cuffey. Until Shirley had become an essential means of transport he had kept her going with oats, and he still stabled her. For Mr Cuffey (though a grimly married man who had never been out of Suffolk in his life, and regularly taking the collection at a Methodist Chapel) had a romantic streak in his nature which made him the slave of Mrs Sheridan's black eyes, purple velveteen trousers, and *haute école* graces. At dusk Mr Cuffey would materialise to woo Mrs Sheridan with illegal cream and extra butter, and sometimes a nice little bit of pork, and sometimes a pheasant which had been foolish enough to get itself entangled in a rabbit snare; and having a generous circus-like outlook on windfalls, Mrs Sheridan would share these courtesies with Midge and Lettice and Justina.

Arriving on the heels of his telegram, Midge's William found himself being conducted, as it were, on a tour through the Sheridans: Mrs Sheridan, Pamela, Gloria, and Roy Sheridan, Driver Sheridan (by proxy of photographs and such a wonderful likeness to the boy), the Alsatian and the horse. But unfortunately he had come on a day which was not the morrow of one of Mr Cuffey's more impassioned dusks.

'If only we had known you were coming, we could have feasted you on the wages of sin,' remarked Midge. 'As it is, it must be fish.'

'I expect William gets a lot of fish in the Navy,' said Justina. 'I expect he's sick of fish. Midge, come outside one minute.'

William heard some serious murmurings, and the sound of damp, flat objects being turned over. Then they reappeared.

'Darling, I'm afraid it won't be fish after all. You see, Justina brought back what she could get, and what she could get was one largish sole and a plaice. And we were to share the sole and Mrs Sheridan was to have the plaice. She prefers plaice. But the sole isn't big enough for three, and if we had the plaice too there would be no fish for Mrs Sheridan. So we think she had better have the sole and we'll have toasted cheese.'

Justina said: 'Fortunately there's quite a lot of cheese.'

'My only criticism is, that you don't seem to have accounted for the plaice,' said William.

'Oh, Mrs Sheridan will have it for her breakfast.'

'She likes plaice, she likes it better than sole,' Midge said. 'It would be a shame to deprive her of her plaice.'

'Especially as she will have been so obliging about the sole,' added Justina.

At breakfast (tea, toast, apple jelly, and the smell of Mrs Sheridan's plaice) and at intervals during the rest of his leave William Corby reminded himself that it is ridiculous to think much about food, that by virtue of his profession he was better fed than any civilian, that it was very handsome of Mrs Sheridan to share the wages of sin with his daughter as well as with her own children, and that it was marvellous for his Midge to have a cook. If she had not got a cook, Midge explained, she would never have time to make so much jam. Midge's jams seemed to be the mainstay of every meal;

though this, as Midge also explained, was partly because if you made jam without as much sugar as the book said, it had to be eaten down immediately or it mildewed.

On Sunday, too, he got a little riding, as Mrs Sheridan lent him her horse.

'But oughtn't she to have a rest?'

'My Shirley is a professional horse. She's never missed a performance, bless her!' said Mrs Sheridan, who, as it was Saturday evening, had an agreeable odour of gin about her.

The Alsatian and the two poodles came along too, and killed and ate several rabbits. Justina's Tom, so he had heard, was a good shot. Every man, thought William, at any rate every husband, should be able to shoot; and he reproached himself that he was incapable of shooting anything except stationary bottles at fairs. One is not a good shot unless one can shoot something edible. He would like to meet Tom Debenham and have some shooting lessons. It would be fun if Tom's next leave should coincide with a leave of his own. It might mitigate, too, this disquieting impression of having four children at Badger Cottage, and two, or possibly three, wives. Yet democracy is desirable; we must all aim at a future of more equality and less formality, and the household at Badger Cottage was a step towards such a future. It was probably reactionary of him to dislike seeing so much of Mrs Sheridan's purple trousers and never feeling sure whether it was Lettice wearing Pamela's rompers or Gloria clasping Lettice's teddy bear who needed picking out of the pond. If he had spent the last three years at home instead of at sea, he would be better at recognising his own child. Meanwhile, he was riding Mrs Sheridan's horse, and Lettice and Midge were sharing in Mr Cuffey's love-gifts, and the joint households of early Soviet days must have been more ill-assorted and infinitely hungrier.

These reflections were cut short by the necessity for galloping across a field in order to deter the two poodles from pulling down a sheep. The fact that the Alsatian had taken no part in this assault but was virtuously engaged in hunting another rabbit was a further reminder that it is the more privileged classes who have most to learn in the matter of citizenship.

Badger Cottage was going on much as usual when a parcel came for Midge containing a large tin of olives and a note from William hoping that they might come in handy. As going on much as usual meant just then that Roy and Lettice had whooping cough and that Gloria had eaten the greater part of an indelible pencil, Midge remarked that dear William must be at Gibraltar, didn't Justina think, and the tin of olives was put by in the store cupboard. Midge was too loyal to voice the wish that William had sent tinned salmon instead, Justina was too polite to say so either, and Mrs Sheridan only said: 'Well, thank God it's in a tin, anyway. Which reminds me, Midgie, my twins have got at the jam you put up in the attic; at first I thought it was mice, but it's too sticky for mice.'

It might have been expected that Tom, coming on leave so soon after this, would have eaten the olives. William had allowed for it. Besides having heard that Tom was a good shot, he had heard that Tom was something of an epicure; and he had said to himself a trifle wistfully: 'To each according to his need' – being, as his father-in-law said, a damn sight too well up in all that anti-God sort of stuff. Tom did not eat the olives because, after his first meal, during which Gloria sat on his knee, toyed with his hair and addressed him with purple lips as Daddy, he announced that he was going to take Justina to London to see some shows and have her nails cleaned.

Driver Sheridan, on the other hand, entered at once into the spirit of Badger Cottage, arriving with a goose, twenty-four kippers, several tins of army stew, two bottles of whisky, four hundred cigarettes, six yellow dusters, and an invaluable collection of nails, screws, belts, and washers, the property of HM Government. During his stay he undertook a number of repairs and improvements, mended the meat safe, washed and clipped the poodles, lifted the maincrop potatoes several weeks too early, repainted the dog kennel and part of the front door, hung a swing for the children, fixed an aerial to the wireless, and did things to the pump. On his last evening, too, he further asserted himself as a practical man by fighting Mr Cuffey, and spent the remaining hours alternately beating and embracing Mrs Sheridan. Bruised and admiring, she passed the next day wandering among his incompleted works, saying dreamily: 'There'll be something to show for this, I shouldn't be surprised.'

The first perceptible aftermath of Driver Sheridan, however, was the cessation of cream and butter, and Mr Cuffey's inability to go on stabling Shirley; never in all his days had he known such a messy horse. It is difficult to place a full-sized horse with delicate lungs: circus life, as Mrs Sheridan explained, the draughts playing on open pores, always weakens the lungs – think of monkeys. Finally, Shirley was accommodated at the Vicarage, where the sound of the organ, said Mrs Sheridan, would be like old times to her. Justina more moodily remarked that she would now be more than a mile from her essential means of transport, and that the Transoms would henceforth expect a regular supply of prizes for their incessant Church Roof Restoration Fund whist drives – as was indeed the case.

Other tokens of Driver Sheridan's manliness were still lying around when William came on his next leave: festering heaps of wood and wire that only needed a few finishing touches to become a rabbit hutch, rusty bolts and cogwheels which should have been put back in the mangle, but somehow got overlooked, and several fresh neuroses in the pump.

'Come just when you're wanted,' said Mrs Sheridan warmly. 'You sailor-men are always so handy.'

If he had not been so obliteratingly in love with his wife, William Corby would have remembered to arrive as a good provider. As it was, he just got into the first train with nothing more than love, lemons, silk stockings, presents for the children, and good intentions. The presents for the children were eaten in a flash, the stockings were put away, love is always impalpable, one cannot live on lemons – he did as best he could with the good intentions. There was certainly a great deal to do. It seemed to him that Badger Cottage was much dirtier and more disarrayed than the passage of six months and the transit of Driver Sheridan could justify. But then, as he told himself, he came off a ship, a childless, melancholy world of its own. Four children would no doubt make a destroyer look as tousled as Badger Cottage; and he thrust down the inward retort to this, that children on a destroyer would be kept in better order and cleaned at regular intervals.

Women, he also told himself, are less fussy than men: it is a wise, natural provision to fit them for the inevitable mess and confusion of maternity. Women, too, are braver, more adaptable, probably hardier, certainly less self-indulgent. They are more primitive and so better attuned to the primitive state of the universe when, as the scriptures so acutely remark, the earth was without form, or void, and the waters brooded on the face of the earth; which reminded him he must try to do something about the bathroom. But the brave, adaptable, hardy, self-disciplined and primitive Midge had spots on her chin, moaned in her sleep, and smoked more than was good for her. As for Justina, she had a cold in her head. It was so violent that she did not go to work, so instead Mrs Sheridan rode into town and did the shopping. Mrs Sheridan was a somewhat erratic shopper, but she always remembered the children; and it was so nice for her, Midge pointed out, to be reunited with Shirley. To give Mrs Sheridan more time to enjoy this reunion, Justina cooked. Justina had been taught cooking at a domestic college for young ladies. She knew how to make omelettes, fudge, several kinds of *soufflé*, coffee, and – theoretically – soap. Unfortunately omelettes and *soufflés* cannot be made without breaking real eggs, so Justina's home-lore chiefly expressed itself in coffee. For the rest there was always cheese, and Midge's jams, and the national loaf, now so vitaminous that it was almost as ready to ferment as the jams. Why on earth, thought William, didn't I have at least the foresight to bring them some ships' bread? Busy himself as he might in being a man about the house, his thoughts dwelt increasingly on food. But he did not realise how enchained he was to sensual lures till the message came from Mrs Transom to say that after all she could not have them to supper as the vicar had just gone down with mumps.

'Mumps! O my God,' wailed Midge. 'None of them has had mumps! O Justina, why did we let them go to the children's service?'

(Mumps, thought William. I've had mumps. I could perfectly well have gone to that supper.)

'I expect he was in his pulpit all the time,' replied Justina. 'It isn't as if he'd been confirming them or christening them. And somebody had to go to church after they'd been so obliging about Mrs Sheridan's horse.'

Damn Mrs Sheridan, thought William.

'What's mumps?' asked Mrs Sheridan; and answered herself by adding that mumps was all in the day's work. She could afford to be philosophical, thought William: she had not lost a supper, she had been staying at home anyway to look after the children. Which, of course, was very good of her.

Justina remarked that there was still quite a lot of the beetroot soup left. Midge said she didn't wonder. William didn't wonder either.

'And there is any amount of oatmeal. Isn't there something called brose that's made of oatmeal – with cabbage in it? Didn't Robert Burns sup brose?'

Mrs Sheridan opined that there was more than that in Robbie Burns' brose.

'What a pity we gave the remains of the rabbit to the dogs!'

The word *olives* began to shape itself in William's mind, but he said nothing.

'It's the very devil,' mused Midge, 'feeding the dogs. They're much fussier than the children. Or us.'

'They don't appreciate the war, poor things,' said Mrs Sheridan. 'Do you think a jam roly-poly? That would be filling. And we must browse down that elderberry jam that wouldn't set.'

The word *olives* now thundered in William's brain. His tongue was swollen with keeping silence. Some flash of his electrical agony must have reached Justina, for suddenly her face became illumined with intellect, and she said:

'I know! I've got it! We'll open that tin of olives that William sent us.'

'O Justina, we can't! It's gone.'

'Gone? Have those blasted children . . .'

'No, it's not the children this time. It's me. I gave it to the Transoms for a whist-drive prize.'

She spoke to Justina exactly as the conventional wife confesses to her husband that she has given his trousers to the jumble sale. Amid everything else that he was feeling, William was able to notice this.

'Damn! What on earth came over you? No one in this village would know what to do with an olive.'

'But you don't like them, Justina. I'm not all that fond of them, really. And Zoe doesn't like them either, for I asked her.'

'I can *eat* them,' said Mrs Sheridan.' But that's not to say I actually enjoy it.'

Midge lit another cigarette. She was still looking like a guilty wife and spoke savagely.

'What else could I do, Justina? You know how those blackmailing Transoms hound us for their whist drives. It's all very well for you, you are out all day, you don't know much about real life. But I can assure you, what with thinking about food for the dogs, and washing for the children, and prizes for the Transoms, real life isn't worth living!'

The ensuing silence was broken by Roy Sheridan, who strolled in carrying a tin chamber pot in which there were some baby mice. He had found the mice in Daddy's rabbit-hutch, he explained. There had been lots more, but they had got away. Now could he have some cotton wool to make a nest for them? Presently William was able to suggest that, since they could not sup at the vicarage (where at this moment, he said to himself, those Transoms are devouring olives like quails and manna), they should walk the four miles into town and have dinner at The Griffin and try for a bottle of whisky for Justina's cold . . . that is, if Mrs Sheridan would stand by her generous offer to keep an eye on the children. It was a lovely frosty night, the walk would be fun.

'We shall get up our appetites,' he concluded.

Mrs Sheridan was quite ready to stay at home, so William set out with his two wives.

The dinner and the whisky cost in all four pounds seventeen shillings. Both Midge and Justina got slightly drunk and were much improved by it. In fact, it might have been called a successful evening if it had not been riddled by a tendency to remember Mrs Sheridan and feel how unselfish she was, and what a pity it was that she had been left out of it.

DAPHNIS AND CHLOE

25 March 1944

Dingy with fatigue, but still kindly, the old waiter glanced from time to time at the weather-beaten boy in mufti, the girl with a blue ribbon in her heaped-up hair, architectural as a peruke. When they came in he had snuffed the odour of mothballs, thinking: It's his first night on leave. Now as they sat on over their emptied coffee cups he thought: A bit of a tiff. Soon blow over.

'But I want to dance with you. All this time I've been looking forward to dancing with you.'

'Dance? What about those dances in the village hall? You won't grow mouldy for lack of dancing, my boy.'

'It's you I want to dance with.'

'Even if we went,' she said, 'I couldn't dance. My knees would be knocking against each other at every step. And I won't go to the pictures, either. One's as dangerous as the other. If you're so bent on dancing, why not dance at home?'

'Round and round the old aspidistra,' he said, 'while your Dad winds the gram. and your Mum does a *pas seul* of her own, looking for where she left her spectacles. And then if a bomb drops on us we won't be killed, because we're not at a Palais de Danse.'

'Well . . . why not drop in at Vanda's? She'd love to see us.'

'Sure she would. Vanda'd love to see a deaf mute with smallpox, she keeps such dazzling company. No! When I get leave I want to see life, not Vanda.'

'See life? See death, more likely.'

'But it's no more dangerous to go to a dance hall than to stay at home. Why can't you see that? God knows I've explained it often enough. It's simply a question of density.'

'I may be dense. But I do know what I'm talking about, and if you'd been through as many raids as I have you'd know too. But that's the trouble. You sit on your blasted heath cuddled round your searchlight and know no more about what it's like in London than a Siamese kitten that's never left Siam.'

With a hand that shook with temper she tilted the coffee pot above her cup. The coffee pot was empty.

'I don't mean that sort of density,' he said carefully. 'I mean density of population. The number of people in a given place. Obviously, in a dance hall there are more people to the square yard than there would be in somebody's quiet home further up the street.'

'It looks like it. A girl I met – she's in ARP and knows what she's talking about – she told me that at Putney they dug out three hundred. I don't know if they were to a square yard or not. But they were for the graveyard all right, what was left of them.'

'But because there are more people in a place it doesn't mean that they are more likely to be killed. It just means that if they are killed there are more of them. Think of it like plates,' he continued. 'Suppose you had fifty plates . . .'

'Why not suppose I had fifty bananas while we're about it?'

'. . . and that you put twenty-five of them in a heap in the sink and distributed the other twenty-five in ones all over the floor. . . .'

Her laughter was as pretty as lambs playing. Hearing it, the old waiter looked round with a smile, and thought: That's all right again!

'. . . and then the little boy next door threw a cricket ball in at the window. If it pitched in the sink, twenty-five plates would be broken; if it hit the floor, only one or two plates, or perhaps none at all.'

Her laughter had ceased. She stared at a mark on the tablecloth.

'Well, it's the same with bombs. It just depends where a bomb falls. Or when it falls. If it falls on a dance hall or a cinema, it may kill three hundred. If it falls on a detached villa called Chatsworth, it may kill three. If it falls on a church on Sunday, it may kill fifty. If it falls on the same church on a Monday, it won't kill anyone.'

'Oh, won't it? You should have seen what they took out of the crypt of Saint Jude's. That was a Monday.'

'I mean a church without a crypt!' he exclaimed. 'But you won't even try to understand.'

'I understand all right. I heard what you said. If a bomb falls on a dance hall, it kills more people. That's why we're not going to a dance hall.'

'But that's not what I said.'

'It is! Only word of sense you've said this evening; it's not likely I shouldn't notice it.'

'I did *not* say it!'

'You did! You said that if a bomb falls on a dance hall more people are killed.'

'But only because more people are there. Look here! If a . . .'

'Well, I don't intend to be one of them. And I don't intend you to be one of them either. I don't want to see you killed. I can't stop you being in the army and I can't stop the war. But I can stop you from marching into death traps, and I mean to. I don't know why you should be so anxious to get us both dead, either.'

'But . . .'

'Personally, I still want us to keep alive, and have a proper home and a family and some fun after all this misery.'

'O God!'

'I don't understand your tony ideas about suicide. I never . . .' She broke off, swallowed violently, and made another attempt with the coffee pot.

'Here, waiter! Another coffee for two, please.'

'Yes, sir. Immediately, sir.'

'No hurry at all,' he said.

Across the little table they stared at each other with murder in their eyes.

ARSACE, IL FAUT PARTIR

c. June 1944

Growing old, the body develops imperious idiosyncrasies, and for some years Odette de Boulay's body had obliged her to get up in the middle of the night and go to the orchard. The usual receptacle, said her brother Yves, would have sufficed any other woman. But not Odette. Odette must needs promenade herself like the Ankou, like a portent of death. At first there had been a show of pretexts, footsteps near the hen house, the bull rattling his chain. But pretexts had been cast aside, the habit became a habit and nothing could alter it, not even the quartering of two occupying lieutenants.

'Now at least you will behave like a reasonable woman! You'll be arrested. You'll be shot.'

'On the contrary. I shall tell them I suffer from insomnia. They won't be able to say anything,' she added derisively. 'They are too correct.'

And indeed since they were under orders to behave as correctly as possible, and since Mademoiselle was the aunt of Clovis de Boulay, nothing was hinted or done to restrict the visits to the orchard. The two lieutenants, the captain who followed them, the chaplain who followed the captain, even the Todt personage who settled in as unobtrusively as a mildew, all correctly knew and correctly admired the regional novels of Clovis de Boulay, novels so expressive of the true, the traditional spirit of France.

Habit persists, subjugating the will that first abetted it, habit becomes a ghost stalking through the deserted manor of the body. In her seventy-third year Odette might think better of an indoor chamber pot; but habit clawed her into the orchard where the winter frosts (though in the Cotentin the frosts are not so severe as those inland) were scarcely less chilling than the heavy dews of summer.

Now it was June. In another three months the apples would be falling. But many would fall before then, shrivelled and useless. It would be a bad apple year, the Ice Saints had come at their sharpest, and now it was not possible to ward off the spring frosts with bonfires. However carefully one covered the fire it might burst into flame and become a signal to the English bombers. So there would be few apples this year. Meanwhile, the weather was changing. A wind swung the boughs, there was rain in the air, the moon. . .

Inattentively, she glanced up to examine the moon. A cloud encompassed it. Only by force of habit interested in the moon she continued to stare at the cloud, which had a rim that recalled to her the ermine tippet she had worn in the first decade of the century. Laid aside in 1914 it had got the moth. Only out of the tail of her eye did she become aware of something in the reinette apple-tree, a something, a bulk.

With half of her mind she thought, a clump of mistletoe. Mistletoe grew well in the orchard, before this war they had made quite a good sum of money sending mistletoe to England for the Christmas market. Naturally, that was now at an end.

With the other half of her mind she thought that Yves would not live to see another Christmas.

It was odd that she had not noticed so large a clump of mistletoe before. No! It was not so odd. The mistletoe was a man.

A man was entangled in the tree. And now this noise which she had taken to be in her head, for she was rheumatic and suffered considerably from head noises, was plainly the wind fidgeting in an extraordinary sort of drapery that depended from the tree.

That was it! He had come down by parachute and had entangled himself in the reinette. She had sometimes foreseen such a thing happening, and now it had happened. He might have chosen a better place. She walked up to the tree, treading on swathes of cold silk, waited a little, said, 'Well?'

There was no answer. She put up a hand and took hold of his foot and pulled at it experimentally. It yielded with the meekness of what is newly dead and still in the limbo between the validity of life, the rigidity of death.

She sighed – a sigh of relief. Presently she began to climb into the tree, hauling herself from bough to bough, carefully not touching the young man who reposed lopsidedly in the heart of the old reinette. At last, leaning along a bough, she was able to look down on his face. It was a young face, in no way remarkable until the moon, poking out of her ermine tippet, looked down too, and gave it a romantic intensity and delineated quite clearly the lappet of blood she had first supposed to be a lock of hair.

What a long way to come in order to lie dead in the old reinette! For he was an American.

They needn't have all this good silk, was her next thought. Yards and yards of silk, and that Herr Kummer sending it off to become chemises for his fat daughters in Saxony. A knife! Doubtless the young man would have a knife on him, and that would save her the trouble of going back for a knife from the kitchen. A knife was strapped to his leg – a long killing knife. He had descended, not to escape death but to inflict it. A piece of metal had interposed between him and his intention. But the others, who had come with him – young men, so armed, coming down by parachute, do not come alone.

Here, beside her in the tree, was the invasion! She began to sidle backwards along the bough, making her way to the ground. Various impulses shook her: to run into the hiding, to escape, to hide for her life; to run back to bed and pull the bedclothes over her ears; to run, not to her own bedside, but to that of Kummer's, the knife in her hand. But instead she fell on her knees, leaning her grey head against the lichened tree, clinging to its bole with all her force.

It had come, and she dared not receive it. It was too much for her, she was too old, too much disheartened. It had come too late. She could not readjust herself, now, in her seventy-third year and in the fourth year of dishonour. She could not readjust herself to liberty. It was too late, she had made her choice and could not unmake it. For one has to choose, and if one is a woman one cannot choose for oneself. There had been Yves, sickly, always dying, asking only to die in peace. There had been the property. There had been the Germans, inescapably victorious, inescapably correct, and appreciating Clo-Clo's talent as his own countrymen had never appreciated it. And there had been Clo-Clo.

'Not that I thought anything of his books,' she exclaimed, addressing the dead soldier's boot. 'All that nonsense about nature and the soil! If he had stayed on the place he'd have learned better. But apparently, it was all he could do.

'And I brought him up, he was like my own child,' she said to the boot.

A child in his forties, still dependent, still needing pocket-money, still sending home his linen to be washed, his socks to be mended, his dialect passages to be corrected, becomes a burden; and even, it seems, becomes aware of becoming a burden. Clovis had drooped, had pined, had written of the heartlessness of Paris and the quiet of country cemeteries, describing himself wistfully brewing tisanes at midnight and thinking of home. Then, in the van of the forces of occupation, Clovis arrived: flushed, dimpled, annunciatory, a little breathless. 'Like a zephyr,' as Yves remarked. At last, he said, embracing her, at last he was in a position to show his gratitude. Henceforth she and Uncle Yves could depend on him.

'It will be difficult to transport Yves,' she had said. 'He went to England once, a town called Worthing, and disliked it.'

The zephyr stiffened. It was not, he explained, a question of flight, and above all not a question of England. The hour had struck for France to embrace her new career as a collaborator in the new Europe. His dear relations would continue to live quietly on their property, setting an example. Honour, comfort, revenue, would flow to them, and he himself would visit them whenever his duties allowed it. For he would be immensely occupied. But even when he could not visit them personally his voice would reach them on the Radio.

'It seems you have everything arranged,' said Yves.

Clo-Clo flickered his hand.

'It is a little in the air. It would be better if you don't talk of it just yet. But the essentials are arranged.'

'I don't like it.' She had said that.

He turned pale, his lips trembled, his eyes became the eyes of a calf dragged to the butcher.

'My career –' His voice rose. 'After all these years of being slighted, of being kept down and reviewed in corners, my career opens. They appreciate me, I tell you. They know my work. They are going to re-issue me in a collected edition. Are you going to wreck me – Now?'

While she hesitated, confused and in anguish, Yves, rearranging the rug over his legs, remarked that it would scarcely be worth it.

'And so – and so,' she murmured, staring at the boot.

So close above her head the boot was enormous. It seemed about to descend, to crush her. Birds flew in and out of the trees, the day was coming, every moment the drapery of the parachute grew paler and its folds more distinct, and she saw that some of it was charred with fire. Holding to the trunk of the old reinette she clambered stiffly to her feet. There was an apple-spray in her hand, for a long time she had been clutching it unconsciously. Now she became aware of it. It was crushed, sodden, done for. She opened her hand and let it fall. Clo-Clo's flourishing career, Clo-Clo himself, and Yves, and she, a flourish put out from an old tree, all done for in this early morning.

She looked at the dead man. He was distinct now, in an hour or so the flies would come buzzing about him. She gave – a courtesy – a thought to the woman who had reared him as she had reared Clovis. A convulsion of misery shook her, but she was scarcely aware of it for in the same moment the air was convulsed by the vibration of heavy gunfire. The parachute fluttered as if it were coming to life. Immature fruit pattered down. It was beginning! It was ending! From long ago, from Paris and her year at the finishing school and the visits in muslin to the Comédie Française, the words, the declamation, the attitude came back to her.

Arsace, il faut partir quand j'aurai vu la reine.

Her cracked voice rang out. She seemed to be standing on an enormous stage. Then, walking rigidly under the tumult of the naval bombardment, she went back to the house.

THE COLD

10 March 1945

The Cold came into the household by Mrs Ryder. At first she said she had picked it up at the Mothers' Union meeting; later – it was the kind of cold that gets worse with time – she attributed it to getting chilled through waiting in the village shop while that horrible Beryl Legg took over half an hour to decide whether she would spend her points on salmon or Spam. Never a thought for her child, of course, who by now should be getting prunes and cereals. Whoever the father might be, one would have expected the girl to show some maternal feeling – but no!

The next person to get The Cold was old Mr Ryder, the Rector's father, and he immediately gave it to old Mrs Ryder. They did not have it so badly, but at their age and after all they had gone through in London before they could make up their minds to evacuate themselves to their son's country parish, one had to put them to bed with trays, just to be on the safe side. Dry and skinny, they lay in the spare room twin beds like two recumbent effigies on tombs, and chattered to each other in faded high-pitched voices. Segregated from the normal family life they had re-established that rather tiresome specialness which sometimes made it difficult to realise that they were really dear Gerald's parents. It is very nice to be cultivated, of course, but somehow in wartime it does jar to labour upstairs with a heavy supper tray and hear, beyond the door, two animated voices discussing Savonarola; and then to hear the voices silenced, like mice when one throws a shoe in their direction, as one knocked on the door and called out brightly, 'Supper, darlings!' and to know, as clearly as if one had seen it, that old Mrs Ryder was stubbing out one of her cigarettes. That jarred, too, especially as she smoked such very heavy ones.

From the old Ryders The Cold descended to the third and fourth generation, to Geraldine and her two boys. Thence it leaped upon the Rector. 'Leaped' was indeed the word. He had set out for the funeral looking the picture of health, he returned haggard and shivering, and so terribly depressed that she had said to herself: 'Influenza!' But it was only The Cold – The Cold in its direst form.

'No!' exclaimed Mrs Allingham, indefatigable secretary of the Women's Institute. '*Not* the Rector?'

'If you had been in church on Sunday you wouldn't need to ask.'

For the indefatigable secretary was a matter for regret on Sundays, when she was more often seen taking her terriers over the Common than herself to Saint Botolph and All Angels. Such a pity! – for in every other way she was an excellent influence.

Recovering herself rather too easily, for it showed that such recoveries were nothing to the rebuked one, Mrs Allingham went on: 'All seven of you! For I can see you've got it too. You poor things! My dear, what do you do about handkerchiefs, now that the laundry only collects once a fortnight? Can I lend you some?'

'Stella washes them.'

'Your marvellous Stella! What would you do without her? I hope she is still standing up.'

'I can't imagine Stella failing us,' said Mrs Ryder with satisfaction.

In the sixth autumn of the war Mrs Ryder was a little tired. She was feeling her age. Her last tailor-made was definitely not quite a success and, say what you will, people do judge one by appearances: she could not help noticing that strangers were not as respectful as they might be; though no doubt the unhelpfulness of Utility corsets played its part in the decline of manners. In the parish, too, there was much to grieve the Rector and the Rector's wife. The old, simple, natural order of things was upset by all these changes, the grocer's son actually a Captain, as much a Captain (and indeed senior in captaincy) as dear Geraldine's Neville, the butcher's wife in Persian lamb, the resolutions at the Parish Council only to be described as Communist, and the girls, her own Girls' Club girls, behaving so shockingly that she often wondered what the mothers of these poor American soldiers would think if they only knew what their sons were exposed to. But she had Stella. And having Stella she had all things.

No one could pick holes in Stella. There were no holes to pick. Stella was physically perfect, not deaf, nor halt, nor imbecile. Stella did not wear glasses and did wear a cap and apron. Stella was functionally perfect, she did not dawdle, she did not waste, she did not gossip, she was clean, punctual, reliable, she was always cheerful and willing, she scrubbed her own back kitchen and mended the choir surplices; and though of course her wages were perfectly adequate, no one could say that the Ryders bribed her to stay with them. Stella stayed through devotion, she could have got twice as much elsewhere. Finally, Stella was a good girl. In a time when manners and morality had gone down alike before expediency, when householders snatched at trousered and cigarette-smoking evacuees if the evacuee would 'help with light domestic duties', when even the houses that ought to set an example employed girls with illegitimate babies and glossed over the capitulation with pretexts of being compassionate and broad-minded, Mrs Ryder continued to boast the ownership of a virgin, a strong womanly virgin who wore skirts, fastened-up unwaved hair in a sensible knob, and said, 'Yes, ma'am.'

Naturally, one took care of such a treasure. Stella's cold was given quite as much consideration as any other family cold and dosed out of the same bottle. In the worst of the epidemic Mrs Ryder said that if Stella did not feel better by midday she really must be sent to bed. For several evenings Mrs Ryder and Geraldine washed up the supper dishes so that Stella might sit quietly by the stove with the surplices instead of shivering in the back-kitchen; and when Stella's cough persisted after the other coughs had died away Geraldine went in specially by bus to look for blackcurrant lozenges and came back with some wonderful pastilles flavoured with horehound.

But it was a long time before Stella's cough could be distinguished from the other coughs by outlasting them. The Cold was such a treacherous type of cold. When you thought you'd got rid of it, it came back. Like beggars, said old Mrs Ryder (for they were downstairs again, one could not keep them in bed indefinitely). Like dandelions, said her son. Geraldine said that she believed it was nutritional. Of course one ought not to complain, the food was marvellous really, more marvellous than ever if one thought about poor old Europe; but still, it wasn't the same, was it? She had met Mrs Allingham, and Mrs Allingham had enquired, of course, about The Cold, and had said that in 1918 everyone had just the same kind of cold, it was quite remarkable. What did the Grand-grands say? Did they have colds in 1918? 'We had much better rum, and more of it,' said old Mrs Ryder. She looked at her husband very affectionately; he stroked his beard and looked back at her, and so they both avoided seeing Mrs Ryder catch her breath like one who holds back a justified reproach because experience has shown that reproaches are vain. The Rector, even more imperceptive, remarked that it was very kind of his parents to make poor Stella a nightcap, he hoped it would do her good. He had seen rum do a lot of good when he was a chaplain in Flanders. Stella was a good girl, a very good girl. They would be badly off without her.

For some reason Mrs Ryder and her daughter now began discussing how tomorrow they really must polish the stair-rods and the bathroom taps. They would make time for it somehow if Mrs Ryder did the altar vases before breakfast and Stella took the boys with her when she went to the farm for milk. If the boys wore their rubber boots, the slush wouldn't do them any harm.

John was five, Michael was three. You couldn't really call them spoilt, they were just wartime, lacking the influence of a father about the house. But not spoilt. Besides, Geraldine liked boys to behave as boys; it would be too awful if they grew up like Neville's ghastly young brother who would sit for hours stroking the cat and turning off the wireless whenever it became worth listening to. A dressing room had been made over as their playroom, but it was bleak up there, and naturally they preferred the kitchen. If anyone spoilt them it was Stella, who didn't seem able to say no to them. And if they were rather fretful just now, it wasn't to be wondered at, it was The Cold.

The doctor's sister, a rather uncongenial character with independent means, used to refer to Mrs Ryder and her daughter as Bright and Breezy. They had a great deal in common, she said, but Geraldine had more of it, and was Breezy. Geraldine now had more of The Cold. Her sneezes were louder, her breathing more impeded, her nose redder, and her handkerchiefs more saturated. Throughout The Cold Mrs Ryder had kept on her feet: as a daughter-in-law, mother, grandmother, and wife to a Rector, she could not do otherwise; but Geraldine had not merely kept on her feet, she stamped and trampled. She scorned precautions, she went everywhere and kissed everybody, just as usual. She did not believe, not she! in cosseting a cold. What are colds? Everyone has them, they are part of English life. Foreigners have things with spots, the English have colds. She made having a cold seem part of the national tradition, like playing cricket and Standing Alone.

And so, when they had all got rid of The Cold and even Stella only coughed at night, Geraldine seemed to be breaking the Union Jack at the masthead when she woke the echoes of the kitchen with a violent sneeze, and asserted:

'I'm beginning another cold. And what's more, I can tell it's going to be a snorter. So watch out, one and all!'

'I do hope not, Miss Geraldine,' answered Stella.

It was rather touching the way Stella still called her Miss Geraldine – as if to Stella the passage of time were nothing, a tide that flowed past the kitchen threshold but never wetted her feet.

'No jolly hope!'

Geraldine went out. Presently she could be heard telling her mother about the new cold. Mrs Ryder sounded unenthusiastic; she said she only hoped it would not last so long this time, as otherwise it would spoil Christmas. Stella went on rubbing stale bread through a sieve for the wartime Christmas pudding. It needed a lot of breadcrumbs; in fact, you might as well call it bread-pudding and be done with it; but Mrs Ryder said the children must be brought up to love Christmas. They stood on either side of the table, rolling bread-pills and throwing them at each other.

The recipe for the wartime Christmas pudding which needed a lot of breadcrumbs also called for grated carrot. When she had finished the breadcrumbs, and put them on a high shelf where she hoped the children might not get at them, Stella went into the back-kitchen and began to clean carrots over the sink. If you rub stale bread through a fine sieve for any length of time, you are apt to develop a pain between the shoulders. She had such a pain; and the change of climate from the kitchen which was hot, to the back-kitchen which was cold, made her more conscious of it. When she had cleaned the carrots she went back to the kitchen. The two little boys were still there and Mrs Ryder had been added.

'Oh, Stella, I came in to say that I thought we would have onion soup tonight, as well as the fish-cakes. Mrs Hartley thinks she has another cold coming on.'

'Yes, ma'am. I wish to . . .'

Mrs Ryder swept on. 'And, Stella, of course I know how busy you are, but all the same I think it would be better *not* to leave the babies alone in here. When I came in I found John playing with the flat irons. Of course they were cold, but they might have been hot. Perhaps a little more thoughtfulness . . . With such young children one cannot be too thoughtful.'

'Very well, ma'am. But I wish to leave, ma'am.'

'Beddy-bies, beddy-bies!' exclaimed Mrs Ryder. 'Come now, John, come, Michael! Kiss dear Stella goodnight, and off with you to your little beds. Now a nice kiss . . .'

'Don't want to,' said the child.

Mrs Ryder seized a child under either arm, waved them in the direction of Stella's face, and conveyed them out of the room, shutting the door on them with a firm sweet, 'God Bless you, my babies!' Then, flushed with exertion, with difficulty withstanding the impulse to go with them, she turned back, hoping that her ears had deceived her and knowing too well that they hadn't.

'I wish to leave, ma'am.'

'Stella! What do you mean?'

'I wish to leave, ma'am.'

There she stood, grating carrots as if the children's Christmas were nothing to her.

'But, Stella . . . I *trusted* you. After all these years! Why, we all look on you as a friend. What has happened to you?'

Could it be, could it be? Stella was short and the kitchen table was high and anything may be happening behind an apron. In a convulsion of the imagination Mrs Ryder rehearsed herself saying that one should not penalise a poor girl for a solitary slip, that kindness, a good home, the example of a Christian home life which means so much, etc, etc. A harlot hope raised its head, and at the same moment she heard Stella say quite idiotically:

'I think I'm catching another cold.'

'Good heavens, girl, is that a reason for going? I've never heard such nonsense.'

'It's nothing but one cold after another – cold, cold, cold, work, work, work! It's not a fit place for me. Both my aunties were chesty, and if I stay here I shall go the same way, I know it. What's more, I'm going tomorrow. I don't mind about my money, I'm going tomorrow. I want to get away while I've still got the strength to.'

'In wartime,' said Mrs Ryder, in her sternest Mothers' Union manner, the manner only unfurled for urgent things like War Savings Rallies and Blood Transfusion Drives, 'in wartime, when our boys are shedding their blood without a moment's hesitation . . . and you are positively running away from a simple cold in the head. I cannot believe it.'

Without a spark of incredulity she banged the door behind her.

There was the Rectory hall. There were the coats and the children's rubber boots and the umbrellas, and the brass letter-tray, and the copper gong, and the stair-rods ascending. There was Gerald writing in his study, and Geraldine gargling in the bathroom, and in the sitting-room the two old Ryders chattering like lovebirds. Here was her home, her dear (except for the old Ryders), her dear, dear home, where everything spoke of love and loving labour: the happy, busy home that was – Mrs Allingham's own words – a beacon to the parish.

But now . . .

Not Stella? Not your marvellous Stella?

The words seemed to dart at her from every side, stabbing through the unsuccessful tailor-made into her ageing flesh. Tomorrow the Sewing Circle met at the Rectory. Only self-respect withheld her from running back into the kitchen to throw herself on Stella's mercy, to beg, on her knees, even, to beg and implore that Stella would change her mind, would stay, would at any rate stay to see them over Christmas. Self-respect was rage and fury. Presently they died down. But she remained in the hall, knowing that any appeal to Stella would be in vain.

Tomorrow the Sewing Circle met. They met at three in the afternoon. Stella would be out of the house before then.

She must be! Mrs Ryder thanked God that self-respect had stood like an angel between her and a fatal false step. 'Stella has gone. Poor Stella! . . . I could not keep her.' A few such words, and a grave grieved silence, nothing that was not true, strictly true; and the Sewing Circle might draw its own conclusions. Cooking, sweeping, scrubbing, doing everything that for so long Stella had done, she could still hold up her head.

POOR MARY

9 June 1945

At the last minute Nicholas remembered flowers. He went out and gathered some primroses from the hedgerow, hardening himself not to notice the snap of their stems. It was one of his fidgets to dislike picking flowers.

The lane sloped away downhill. Here and there the leafless hedge was tufted with white where the blackthorns had come into bloom. It was like a black wave breaking into lips of foam. Down in the valley a white plume of steam rose up, its summit catching the pink light of sunset. It was still hanging there when he heard the train go on. And he knew that his wife, shouldering her pack, had handed in her pass and joined the nondescript civilian group waiting for the bus. The white plume thinned out, the train gathered speed, snorting on towards London. But Mary had got out at East Wickering, junction for Stoat and Saint Brewers.

I want to spend this leave at home, she had written; *unless you'd rather not. It's more than time I saw you in your hermit's cell*. If it had not been for the last sentence he would have supposed she wanted to spend her leave with her family.

'Flowers for the spare room,' he said to himself, setting down the spotted mug in the centre of the bureau. The bed, an old-fashioned double bed with brass endrails and a white quilt, suddenly seemed a bed in which he had never slept. It looked like Wordsworth's bed. He must contrive that she saw the camp bed first. For the last week he had spent his spare time preparing for her, scrubbing the floors, polishing the windows, putting away his clothes, his books, his papers, so that his dwelling might offer its most impersonal face to her inspection. Now that he had remembered flowers everything seemed ready. The food on the table was covered with a napkin to keep flies off it, the kettle was in a state to boil when he wanted it to, the watercress was keeping cold in a damp cloth. He snuffed at his fingers' ends, and once more washed his hands very carefully. He had been cleaning out pigsties all the morning. Then he set off to meet his wife.

He had not seen her since 1941. A conscientious objector, he had applied for exemption from military service. The day after the tribunal had granted him exemption provided he worked on the land, Mary volunteered for the ATS. They had never agreed about war, so neither was surprised by the other.

'But as we are bound to argue,' she had said, 'and people will only laugh at you if you have a military wife coming on visits, I shan't come. Unless you are ill, of course. Then I will apply for compassionate leave.'

One of the things he had learned in four years spent as a farm labourer was an exact computation of time. So he met her where he had intended to meet her, fifty yards from where the bus had set her down at the foot of the lane. Though he knew she would be wearing uniform, it was a surprise to see that part of the uniform was a skirt. He had been similarly astonished on their wedding day when apparently he had been assuming that she would come up the aisle wearing white satin trousers. Seeing the skirt, he also saw her legs below it and that they were fatter than they used to be.

'Hello, Nicholas!'

'Hullo, Mary!'

She smells of metal, he thought, as I smell of dung. We are subdued to what we work in. He had smelt her, he had seen her legs. He did not seem to have seen her face. He took her pack, and said: 'Look! There's a hawk.'

'I suppose they do a lot of harm to the crops,' she replied.

'Wood pigeons are worse.'

She set off, walking with quick resolute steps. Marching, in fact. So why on earth should she know about hawks? The thought prompted an enquiry about the V-2, and they went up the lane talking of air raids and air raid damage. Just as there was a difference between their smells and a difference in their gait, there was a difference in their manner of speech. Her voice had grown rather common and twanging, it sounded uncared-for, and she jumped from one subject to another. She seemed to preface every remark with *Gosh!* and he to inaugurate every reply with *Um*. Listening to himself, he thought: Do I sound more like the village schoolmaster or the village idiot?

A melancholy tenderness that was almost entirely the April dusk suffused him. Blackbirds shot across the path from hedge to hedge, scolding at them; beyond the hedges lambs bleated and rushed away at a ghostly gallop. He had been working from six in the morning; he was tired and craved for tea. Yet each time that they paused for Mary to recover her breath he was glad to postpone the moment of reaching his house, and when the one chimney pot reared into view above the hedge and beneath the evening star he said gloomily: 'Here's where I live.'

'It's nice. And all to yourself? Lucky bastard!'

'There are only two rooms,' he said defensively. 'The third one leaks.'

'Is it old?'

'Run up after the last war by a chicken-farming ex-serviceman. When he was ruined the farmer bought it. As he bought it very cheap, naturally he doesn't trouble to keep it in repair. So I sit in the kitchen. But I've got a chemical closet.'

It was strange to hear her feet on the floor of concrete slabs. Not strange to her, though, who had been living for four years in army constructions. The only strange thing to her would be to hear two pairs of feet instead of thirty. He moved the kettle forward on the range and lit the candles.

'Candles!' she said appreciatively.

'Because it's a party. Ordinarily I use an oil lamp.' His voice was still heavy with gloom.

'What queer squat candlesticks! They're clay, aren't they? Did you make them?'

'No. I bought them at a sale. They're called corpse candlesticks. The idea is that you leave them by the body all night, you see, and the rats can't knock them over.'

'I wonder you don't use them every night,' she said. 'Have you got any other cheerful curiosities?'

She had taken off her cap and unbuttoned her tunic. The candlelight softened the contest between her natural high colour and the too tawny make-up she had applied to it. Seeing that he was looking at her, she said: 'Isn't it calamitous how fat I've grown? It's that army food, incessant gorges of starch. Gosh! Those puddings! Enough to make any girl look like a prize ox.'

'When I first came here I was covered with spots and boils,' he said consolingly. 'I thought I'd caught it from the pigs, till I discovered it was my water well. Now I boil it.'

'I'd hate to have to do with pigs.'

'They're clean animals, really. It's just that they are overcrowded, and dirty feeders.'

'Sounds like the ATS.'

He cut more bread, reflecting that he would need to bake again on the morrow. Habit, of course, and mass-feeding, and the goaded appetite of the disciplined: though that would not account for the scatteration of eggshell, the jam spooned on to a salted plate, the wide periphery of crumbs and cigarette ash. Nerves, he thought. Poor Mary's nerves are strained. His own strained nerves obliged him to sip his tea as though it were Napoleon brandy and frown at an iron-mould on the cloth.

'Lovely bread, Nicholas.'

'Soda bread. I bake it myself.'

'You seem to have a lot of time. Don't you ever do any work?'

'Fifty-six hours a week. Sometimes overtime. Pigs on Sunday. But it fits in somehow, and I don't dislike it. And the alternative would be to have a woman in.'

He had not meant the implication and she did not perceive it. Staring round her as though in a foreign country, she said: 'And the polish on everything, too! You're wasted, Nicholas. You ought to be in the army.'

'Yes, sergeant.'

But, more concerned than he had been over his own maladroit remark, she flushed, and refused to eat anything more, like an abashed child.

'Walk round and see the rest of it. Here's your room.'

'Pretty flowers.'

Glaring at the bed, he remarked: 'I've got a bed in the third room.'

'But that's the room that leaks. You said so.'

She had turned round from the mirror, and it was as though the mirror had given back to her her former countenance, at once innocent and domineering, the face of the girl-child intent on the doll's tea party.

'It doesn't leak in dry weather,' he said. 'I expect the cat's there now. She comes in and out by the window.'

'Cat? Why, you used to hate cats. You said they tortured birds.'

'So they do. So I do hate them. But I must needs find this animal in a gin, and dress its paw, and the damned beast has adopted me. It's a female, too.'

'Life's harder in the country, I expect,' she said. It was for such slanting ironies that he had first loved her: for that, and for smelling of geraniums, and for the chivalrous quarrelsome disposition which had kept her at his side before his exemption was assured, saying hopefully that he might need someone to scrap with the authorities. But unseeing, she went on to undo it by saying: 'You know, a lot of people are awfully interested when I tell them my husband is a CO. You'd be surprised how many feel the same way. All these murder cases, you know. Everyone's dead against the death sentence.'

'It doesn't surprise me very much,' he said. 'I was in the train the other day, I had to go to a dentist. And there was a bomber crew in the same carriage, and they were talking about a murder. They all agreed that it was wrong to take human life. I asked one of them why, and he said because you can't know what it is you're meddling with.'

'Exactly! I've heard dozens say the same thing. I'm beginning to think so myself. I think they ought to abolish it, I expect they will after the war.'

'They'll abolish war, my dear. Belligerents always abolish war after a war. It's harder to part with a death sentence. And impossible to give up hunting and shooting, because hunting and shooting make us what we are. Have a cigarette?'

'I don't think you've grown any pleasanter,' she said. 'Is that an owl? Let's go back to the other room.'

In the other room the clock was ticking, the kettle was boiling. Three hours earlier the bed had not seemed his own, now his kitchen was not his either, but some sort of institutional waiting room where two people had made an inordinately messy meal. At last, irked beyond bearing, he rose and began to clear the table and then to wash up. The hot water in the bowl, the feeling of the crockery, dried and still warm as he stacked it on the dresser, the resumption of his ordinary evening routine began to console him. He moved to and fro more nimbly, preparing for the two breakfasts he would get in the morning, pouring the remains of the tea into the bottle he would carry to work with him – he had grown to enjoy cold tea – rinsing out the teapot and standing it on its head, throwing out the slops and bringing in the kindling for the morrow's fire, winding the clock and putting the cat's saucer down on a sheet of newspaper. Now, had he been by himself, he would have raked out the fire and gone off to read in bed. Instead, hospitality constrained him to say: 'Have you brought a hot-water bottle?'

She did not answer. With a kettle in one hand and the wood basket in the other, he glanced at her. Her head was resting against the back of her chair and her eyes were shut. But she was not asleep. She was openly and abjectly crying.

He built up the fire and put on the kettle. This, whatever it was about, would mean more tea. Then he patted her shoulder and said: 'Poor Mary!' She put up her hand that was so plump and so demonstrably manicured, and clung to his wrist. She's going to have a baby, he thought. The cat in the gin that had clawed him to the bone, clawed and clung, had been within a few days of giving birth. He had made her a nest in the woodhouse, but she had limped off to hide under a gorse-brake. The kittens had grown up and gone their wild way, and now she was pregnant again. But for poor Mary there was nothing but some sort of nursing home.

She clung to his wrist and rubbed her head against his arm. Moulting, he thought, still clinically remembering the cat. She was going to have a baby, no doubt of it. It accounted for everything, for her nerves, for her legs, for her appetite, for her arrival. Poor Mary! Patriotism had not been enough, she had had no hatred in her heart for anybody, and so she was going to have a baby. The fortunes of war. Some get killed, some get maimed, some are got with child. There ought to be a pension from the War Office. And in that dreadful uniform, too, those pitiable skirts turned up. I hope to God, he thought, I shall not have to meet the father – one of those strenuous noodles who think badly of the death sentence as like as not. I'm damned if I will. And the next instant he was thinking: My poor Mary, I hope it wasn't a rape. Meanwhile his indifferent body was complying with the schedule of his daily life, and he felt himself to be growing more and more sleepy, and knew that unless he spoke he might yawn.

'If you'll let go a minute, Mary, I'll make some tea.'

She let go. The hand that had been so strong fell on her lap and crept into the other hand. Presently it moved again and pulled out a khaki handkerchief, and she began to mop her eyes and snort back her tears.

'This damned war! It's this damned war, Nicholas.'

He groaned assentingly.

'Now that it's nearly over, how I hate it!'

With an effort he refrained from pointing out that it was only in Europe that the war might be said to be nearly over.

'If they'd let me fight, as I wanted to, I might be killed by now. If we'd stayed in London and I'd driven an ambulance or a pump I might be killed by now. As it is, I've never been so healthy in all my life.'

'You don't look well,' he said. 'I noticed at once that you looked tired. And you got frightfully out of breath walking up the hill.'

'Fat! My healthy army fat! When I come out of the army, Nicholas, I shall come out healthy, hideous, middle-aged, and without an interest in life. And there will be hordes and hordes of me, all in the same boat. Gosh, what a crew!'

Giving up the hypothesis of a baby, he realised how much he was relinquishing. Once it was born, she would have been happy enough.

'We shall all be in that boat, dear. Besides, you're a sergeant, aren't you? That's something. You'll soon get thin, once you're out in the rough-and-tumble of civilian life. Once you're thin, you'll take hold, you'll get interested in something or other. Probably you'll fall in love, and make a fresh start.'

The kettle was boiling. He began to prepare for more tea.

'Fall in love? Fall in love?' she cried. 'Not again! You see, I did it.'

He paused, kettle in hand. Would nothing rid him of these turbulent kettles?

'And he was killed? I'm sorry, Mary.'

'He wasn't killed. He chucked me, and now he's married to another bitch.'

'And that's all?'

'And that's all.'

He glanced towards the clock. It felt like midnight, but it was only half-past ten. If he could give her something stronger, some whisky, some rum. A little rum, now, in her tea. . . . But a pigeon-shooting party last week had cleaned out The Red Lion of everything except aniseed cordial.

'Sugar?' he enquired.

She looked at him.

'I'm sorry. I'm sorry! I asked you that only three hours ago, didn't I? I am an insensate clod.'

'That's all right, Nicholas. Actually, I never take sugar in tea. You could have had all mine, you see. Think what you've missed. Actually, why I came back was to see if you'd ever want to live with me again. Not that I thought it likely. Why should you? Anyhow, it's plain you don't. So that's over. What good tea you make.'

She drank in gulps, swallowing violently, swallowing tea and tears.

'You were always domestically inclined, weren't you? It will be a comfort to me, yes, really it will, to think of you being so happy and tidy and self-contained, with your cat and your corpse candles and your books and your flowers. Did Robinson Crusoe have flowers on his table, as well as his old cat sitting up to it like a Christian? I can't remember. Perhaps when we are both very old I may come and spend the afternoon with you on your island. And you can make me some of your nice tea, and ask me if I take sugar with it. But of course I'll give you ample warning. I won't be a disquieting footprint. I did warn you this time, you know.'

She had risen. She had picked up her cap and her pack and her cigarette case and her lighter and her lipstick and all her bits and pieces.

‘I think I’ll go to bed,’ she said. ‘I’ve got rather a headache.’

‘Yes. We’ll go to bed.’

Leaving the room all anyhow, he thought, as he stared at her submissive military back in the doorway. Whether it made things better, whether it made them worse, it was the only thing he could do, the only way he could comfort her. They would lie in the Wordsworthian bed, their smells of dung and of metal would mingle, her shoulder would feel like greengages and her hair would get in his mouth, and she would be silent. It was one of her graces that she was silent in bed. And afterwards, when she had gone to sleep, he would straighten himself and lie on his back, letting the day’s fatigue run out of his limbs as the fleas run out of the body of a shot rabbit. And probably his last waking thought would be of the alarm clock, poised to wake him at five-thirty, and of the limpid innocent morning in which he would go out to his work.

THE WAY BACK

c. July 1945

'And on the first of July,' he said, 'I landed in England. And that is the end of my story.

'If it had not been for my parents,' he added, 'I would have stayed in France. In France or in Europe. Somewhere around. You can pick up nationalities off the roadside, any nationality you please, on the roads of Europe today. If I could have been reported dead, I would have stayed; people soon get over a death. But Prisoner and Missing is the devil – my parents would have gone on worrying. So I came back.'

As they walked out of the restaurant he said:

'Do you think I've changed?'

'A great deal,' she answered. 'Your nose is more hooked, your whole physiognomy is changed. You look formidable. It's very becoming.'

Now he began to survey the traffic going westward through the town. The driver of a lorry slowed down and drew in to the edge of the pavement.

'Like a lift, soldier?'

'Bridgwater,' he said, 'or thereabouts.'

‘Take you as far as Somerton.’

‘That’ll do nicely. For while I’m waiting for my medical,’ he said, turning to his companion, ‘I’m putting in time hiking about to all the places I’ve been a misfit in. To find out if it was them or me. Well, goodbye. Thanks a lot for finding me changed.’ A week at home, she thought, was as much as he could stand.

The brewery, the gasworks, the outlying bungalows, fell behind them, and the fat and flourishing landscape imposed its contours on the course of the road. The driver asked: ‘Been back long, soldier?’

‘Fortnight tomorrow.’

‘Germany?’

‘Poland, actually.’

‘Quite a step,’ said the driver. ‘How did you get there? Do you smoke?’ The cigarette was smoked out between Caubourg and Alençon, for to begin with the driver asked questions and imposed glosses from other narratives. Ash trees and hedgerow elms, unimpaired steeples, buildings trim, or sagging under nothing more than senility, flowed towards them, whisked by, were demolished behind them. It was easier to tell his story thus than while sitting in a restaurant eating stewed rabbit. Food should be eaten in silence, anyway, with the savage attention which is its due.

The narrative travelled eastward, was noosed to a standstill, was released and went eastward again, lost its impetus, halted, and turned back.

‘Pity you couldn’t get as far as Moscow,’ said the driver. ‘But I daresay you’ll get there some time. Seems to me if I’d been behind barbed wire and got out again I'd never settle down for long, I'd be afraid to. Shouldn't think you feel altogether like settling down, not at your age.'

'As long as they don't settle me down in some base. . . . Well, thanks for the lift.'

'Thanks for the story,' said the driver. 'Best of luck, I'm sure. Meet you in High Street, China, eh?'

He drove off, the engine noises whacking his empty ears. Oughtn't to dump him in a base, he thought. A week of the old spit and polish would be as much as he could stand.

This time it took the young man longer to pick up a ride, or he was harder to please. Two private cars paused to invite him, but he refused them, saying that he was not going their way. Finally he got into a builder's lorry which was travelling in the same direction. This time he kept his story to himself. Yes, he was just back. No, he had been a prisoner. Yes, it was all right being home. He sat and stared at the oncoming road. The landscape had flattened out, its contours were less imposing, the road seemed able to assert its independence and take a straight course. Where it crossed a muddy little river, shuffling along under willow trees, he halted the driver.

'Going to the camp, are you? Well, you'll see some changes since last time.'

'I can see them from here,' he replied.

The crest of the last low hill was covered with hutments, and hutments sprawled down its flank. They were painted over with a camouflage in tones of stale mustard. But under the milky sunlight of the day the mustard colours suggested some low form of animal life rather than any kind of vegetation. It was as though the hill were covered with a plague of caterpillars – caterpillars which since he had last been here had pullulated a thousandfold. As a distant window tilted towards the sunlight, as a glass-panelled door opened or shut, minute flecks of light flashed out, and it was as though the caterpillars were slightly squirming.

He gave it a long, steady look and then struck off across the meadow, walking on the raised bank of the stream. Even now, in mid-July, with meadowsweet in bloom and dragonflies hawking over the surface of the water, the rushes along the embankment were fastened together with wisps of muddied grass, the tidemark of the winter's floods. The air had a particular smell, wild and pure – the smell of air unbound from the usual tether of hedgerow. As far as he could see before him there were no hedges. Ranks of willows, embanked ditches, sometimes a wire fence, marked the divisions of the land. He was back once more, walking freely where three years before he had walked furtively and defiantly, defending in the teeth of a carefree communal life his personal right to be solitary and full of cares. He was back once more, and the mood of those days rose up and reclothed him, so that he found himself suddenly and intently quickening to forgotten preoccupations, so that the downward sighing of a willow bough became his loathing of a red face adjusting itself to a mouthful of beef, so that a hairy plaster of mud on a post where cows rubbed themselves became his conviction that when he made his first drop, a fly would be drawn into his windpipe and he would land ignominiously stifling.

Now he could see the farm quite clearly, a small, composed building of earth-coloured brick with a hooded porch and a round window above it. It had an air of being tranquilly idle, of sitting with its hands folded among the rabble of barns and sheds and ricks and cowstalls that surrounded it. As one came nearer, the illusion of idleness was lost, the house rang like any other farmhouse with noises of feet, buckets, children, and crockery. But from here it sat with its hands folded, watching the pears ripen on the south wall. But now the charm was lost. It no longer bothered his mind as it had done then, and afterwards in thoughts and in dreams.

He skirted round it. Something else was missing too, something that had been an irritation, a fret. The dog, of course. The dog that had always barked was not barking. Just as he was thinking with pleasure that it must be dead – it had been a most objectionable, unhappy cur, always tied to its kennel, always working itself into hysterics – he caught sight of it, still tied and with the same dirty enamelled bowl still beside it. But this time it was not barking. He shrugged his shoulders and smiled and walked on. One brings back something from one's travels, if only the ability to best an old watchdog on a chain.

Ahead of him in a field alongside the familiar track some men were gathering in the remnants of a crop of rushy hay. He could see the flies round their heads, fetched by the smell of their sweat. He turned off to avoid them. In this level landscape with its foam of meadowsweet, its banks of green willow rippled and tumbling like some real wave thrust up through the sea-level earth, one could walk at random and yet never lose one's bearings. The last time he walked here he had tried, most deliberately tried, to lose himself. But in vain. A group of poplars, a cattle shed, a detail of the horizon, a gated bridge across a drain – there was always something to whistle him back. It would be difficult to be lost even in the whole of England, England is so small; what hope of getting lost on Sedgemoor? – unless one is poor Monmouth.

Monmouth's men had fought with pikes, with clubs, with scythes. In 1940 pikes were issued to the Home Guard, and all the old fire-eating gentlemen went round saying that the pike is a damn fine weapon, sir, and a match for any automatic. Cold steel, sir. . . . Unfortunately Monmouth's men had not found it so. Yet their tactics had been good, taking advantage of the terrain and its morning mists, tying up the royal troops in rhines and ditches. The mistake had been to engage in battle – a mistake generals are particularly prone to; and Monmouth had been Captain-General of the King's forces, enough to ruin any commander. With Maquis methods a long smouldering insurrection might have changed the story of England; though sabotage is not so effective against an enemy who moves on foot and horseback, not by train and lorry, who depends on local industries and not on power stations. Yet the moral effect, the unsettlement, the demoralisation, would have been as great, perhaps even greater, for using the superstitions of the times. . . . And here again he was riding off on the same fallacy, giving King Monmouth's men the mentality of three centuries later, whereas in fact they would have been just as much subject to haunts and witches as their adversaries.

The aspect of a group of willows told him that by inadvertence he had at last achieved his ambition, and was lost. Then he saw a man with a gun come out from among them.

In an instant he was flat on the ground, refuging his human-coloured face and hands behind a tussock of grass. Life rushed into him, he was alive again, and devoted, mind, body, and soul, to living. Lying motionless, his ear to the ground, his muscles striking the brilliant bargain between immobility and the power to leap to his feet in a flash, he felt himself changed from lead to gold.

The man's foot took a step forward. There was a twang, the twang of a single-strand wire fence. A rabbit got up beside him, flicked its ears and ambled towards the sound. There was a crack of gunfire, and he heard the pellets scatter and bounce on the dry ground, and the drumming of the rabbit's feet as it galloped off, and the man's slow voice saying: 'Missed 'un.'

So now he lay still because he had made a fool of himself, and heard the man walk away, pause, and shoot again and walk on. A bad shot, he had not got his rabbit this time either. At last he got up and dusted himself and beat off some ants and looked about him. The group of willows was still strange; but a puff of wind blew the boughs to one side, and through them he saw on the southward skyline the camp in its mustard-coloured camouflage, sprawling and faintly squirming. He was not in the least lost. He had walked in a circle, that was all.

'And I thought I had learned not to do that,' he chided himself as he walked on to meet the main road and his next lift.

MAJOR BRICE AND MRS CONWAY

c. May 1946

In May 1946, Major Brice, of the US Army, revisiting London and liking it no better than before, drove himself into the country on a vernal impulse to re-examine a Mrs Conway who in 1944 had been briefly his hostess and his mistress – and more to his taste in the second category. Her house had been cold, her bathroom had been gaunt, her table had been ill-spread except when he spread it, and from sundown to sunrise he had been pestered with black-out regulations. That was how he had discovered her more satisfactory aspect. For while he lay reading in bed, the only place where he could escape from the draughts, she had burst into his room, wearing of all things a steel helmet – she had been out on some civilian nonsense or other – saying furiously that if he was afraid to go to sleep in the dark he might at least exert himself to draw his curtains properly. As one throws a cover over canaries when they make too much noise, he had switched off the light while she was still in mid-career. *Oh!* she had said, startled into primness. A minute later she and her helmet were scattered on his bed.

And really, that was the thing he most warmly remembered: her startled *Oh!* so inadequate and female, her lips, fresh with the outdoor cold, and the genuine satisfaction of having silenced them.

That was in February or early March. Ten days later he had gone off to a battle school and after that to battle itself. 'Give my regards,' he had said, 'to your English spring.' Every dreary acquaintance of hers and her incessant sister-in-law incessantly had remarked to him that really he should see Ludworth in an English spring.

Now, as the lanes became familiar and the names he had known by ordnance map and hearsay appeared on the fingerposts – Abbot's Woolcombe, Little Poakers, Chelbury Regis – he was seeing it. There was too much of it, he thought, and all of it too close. Hawthorn hedges blocked his way like snowdrifts, the small, steep pastures were bruisingly vivid with buttercups, and when he paused to study yet another fingerpost at yet another junction of floral rat-runs, the noise of the birds was deafening as musketry, and the smell of the may-blossom made him sneeze. She had been much the same, he thought: her lust too lusty, her abandonment without sensibility; and all, like this landscape, in such a small way; for there had been no perspective of love between them, no basic tenderness, scarcely a farewell, and no letter-writing. She had bestowed herself as the English sell bread: unwrapped and unanalysed.

As the house came into sight he thought: Perhaps she is away; and the surmise was followed by a distinct sense of relief. He wanted her to be away. But for all that he drove in between the stone gateposts and got out, leaving his bag in the car, and rang the bell.

The door was open, he could see into the house. It was as shabby as ever, so shabby that one could not see that it was two years the shabbier. After a while, since no one answered the bell (no one had ever answered any bell, for the only house-servant was stone-deaf), he walked in and went into the sitting room. Nothing was changed yet everything was different. Presently he saw why. The hearth on which she had kept so inadequate a fire was blazing with sprays of beech and laburnum, with white irises and fat crimson pæony blossoms. The faded green walls, the sheep-faced family portraits, the exhausted upholstery, were shadows in a garden; for trophies of flowers stood everywhere, and through the open window the branches which had rapped with wintry fingers on the pane extended into the room – mock-orange and clematis and sagging roses.

Except for the birds yelling outside, all was silent. When he could bear it no longer he turned on the wireless. Out came a talk on the cuckoo. He twiddled until he found some dance-music, and made it as loud as possible. That always used to fetch her, then.

It fetched her now. She went by outside the window, wearing a blue dress. He whistled her. She made an almost imperceptible turn of the head, but did not pause.

When she had not come in he began to feel somehow alarmed. He switched off the wireless and heard her steps go swiftly along the passage. Then a door shut. That was all. He snapped on the wireless again, and the small action transmuted his feeling of alarm into anger and resentment. This was their English hospitality!

Unheard, she was in the room, wearing a green dress and saying: 'Do you mind if I turn this down a bit?' just as she used to do. Then she turned it off, just as she used to do, and advanced on him with her ugly, inattentive smile, the smile of a street urchin and not a woman's smile at all, and held out her hand, and said:

'Hullo! how nice to see you.'

Her voice expressed nothing beyond being in her own house and addressing someone who had entered it. But for all that she had stayed to change her dress. Her hand was quitting his when he took a firmer hold of it and kissed it. It was pretty much like kissing a lizard – a lizard with some ill-fitting rings on.

'Are you over here for long? Do sit down and tell me all your adventures. Did you enjoy the war?'

Aching to slap her face, he settled back in a chair, crossed his legs, lit a cigar, and said:

'Well, it was interesting. I suppose it would have been even more interesting if one had known it was in the nature of a last performance.'

'Do you think so?'

'Well, there aren't going to be any more wars like that. All that's a back number, now.'

'Oh, of course. You're thinking of your new bomb.'

'I'm not the only one who's doing that.'

'And do you know all about it, Terence?'

'No. We don't let it out quite as freely as that.'

'What a shame! Never mind, perhaps you'll be allowed to drop one. On London, for instance. You'd love that.'

'I mightn't feel too badly about it,' he said. 'But I wouldn't be doing it, anyway. They'll probably come over by rocket.'

'Better and better,' she said. 'Why, in the next war you Americans won't need to put yourselves out at all.'

'No. We'll just be sending you parcels. As usual.'

He looked at her green dress. It was ugly, made of a poor stuff and coloured with a poor dye. She had looked better in the blue one. Being a man of thoughtful character, he reflected: Suppose she went and changed into an uglier dress because of me? If she imagined it enhanced her green eyes, she was wrong. It put them out.

'As a matter of fact,' he said, 'I just came down to look at the village church.'

She laughed.

'Suppose you have some tea first.'

'Oh, tea!' But because she had laughed and for a moment had looked easy, he added: 'Well, I'd like to eat another of those things like sponges. Crumpets.'

'But one doesn't eat crumpets in May!'

She spoke with no more malice than a schoolteacher, and nothing she had said before was comparable as an insult.

'Of course not, of course not! It's their mating season.'

She waited a moment or two, and said smoothly:

'You're looking very well, Terence. Did you come over by air or on a food ship?'

He threw his cigar at the pæonies and got up, just in time to see her walk into the room wearing a blue dress.

'Mary, this is Major Brice. This is my daughter, Terence.'

Mary Conway was not a beauty, she had no style, she had nothing beyond the temporary advantage of being twenty years younger than the mother she so exactly resembled. So why should Ruth Conway sound so jubilant about her? She could not possibly know of his mind's slight misadventure with a blue dress.

'Major Brice has come down from London to see the church, darling. He hadn't time to see it when he was quartered here in 1944.'

'I suppose you were frightfully busy?'

'Frightfully.'

Twenty years ago Ruth Conway was just as obtuse, no doubt. But now, he reflected, she wasn't. Such a situation had possibilities.

'After tea you must show it to him.'

'Oh, yes, I'd love to. Do you like architecture, Major Brice?'

'I'm fascinated by your British architecture.'

'He's seeing all he can in the time,' remarked her mother.

'I suppose you are going back quite soon?'

'We Americans are always in a hurry, you know. We haven't got your background, we haven't got your sense of repose.'

She turned to her mother and said: 'Would you like me to do anything about hurrying tea?'

'Don't think about tea,' he said. 'I know how things are over here. I'd hate to take the jam sandwiches out of your mouths. It's just the church I want to see.'

'Make sure he signs the visitors' book, Mary.'

‘I’m crazy about your old village churches. We have no churches in the States, you know.’

‘I expect you come from the Middle West,’ said the girl. ‘You ought to visit New England. There are some very nice churches in New England. They are made of wood and painted white, and they look exactly as if Sir Christopher Wren had designed some rather grand bathing machines for Queen Anne. They can be moved about on rollers, too, which is more than you can say for our churches here. You really ought to go to New England if you are so fond of churches.’

‘Don’t the New Englanders speak with quite an accent?’ asked the son of Vermont.

‘Yes, they do, rather. It’s supposed to be an English accent really. In some of the backward places in Lincolnshire the old people still talk like that.’

‘Your mother didn’t tell me you’d visited our country.’

‘I was sent there in 1940 to be out of the way. I was there for two years, and I came home with a collection of the wildest hats, and such an accent that Daddy sent me to school all over again to be scraped.’

With a picture in his mind’s eye of how Ruth Conway must be enjoying herself, he glanced round to confirm it. She was kneeling before the hearth. So she had knelt before, puffing at the fire with a pair of wheezy bellows and sometimes even dimly apologising for the absence of central heating; but now she was tranquilly rearranging her pæonies.

His weekend bag, he remembered, was still in his car. He was in two minds whether it shouldn’t remain there.

Persephone Books publishes the following titles:

No. 1 *William – an Englishman* (1919) by Cicely Hamilton
No. 2 *Mariana* (1940) by Monica Dickens
No. 3 *Someone at a Distance* (1953) by Dorothy Whipple
No. 4 *Fidelity* (1915) by Susan Glaspell
No. 5 *An Interrupted Life: the Diaries and Letters of Etty Hillesum 1941–43*
No. 6 *The Victorian Chaise-longue* (1953) by Marghanita Laski
No. 7 *The Home-Maker* (1924) by Dorothy Canfield Fisher
No. 8 *Good Evening, Mrs. Craven: the Wartime Stories of Mollie Panter-Downes 1939–44*
No. 9 *Few Eggs and No Oranges: the Diaries of Vere Hodgson 1940–45*
No. 10 *Good Things in England* (1932) by Florence White
No. 11 *Julian Grenfell* (1976) by Nicholas Mosley
No. 12 *It's Hard to be Hip over Thirty and Other Tragedies of Married Life* (1968) by Judith Viorst
No. 13 *Consequences* (1919) by EM Delafield
No. 14 *Farewell Leicester Square* (1941) by Betty Miller
No. 15 *Tell It to a Stranger: Stories from the 1940s* by Elizabeth Berridge
No. 16 *Saplings* (1945) by Noel Streatfeild
No. 17 *Marjory Fleming* (1946) by Oriel Malet
No. 18 *Every Eye* (1956) by Isobel English
No. 19 *They Knew Mr. Knight* (1934) by Dorothy Whipple
No. 20 *A Woman's Place: 1910–1975* by Ruth Adam
No. 21 *Miss Pettigrew Lives for a Day* (1938) by Winifred Watson
No. 22 *Consider the Years 1938–1946* by Virginia Graham
No. 23 *Reuben Sachs* (1888) by Amy Levy
No. 24 *Family Roundabout* (1948) by Richmal Crompton
No. 25 *The Montana Stories* (1921) by Katherine Mansfield
No. 26 *Brook Evans* (1928) by Susan Glaspell
No. 27 *The Children Who Lived in a Barn* (1938) by Eleanor Graham
No. 28 *Little Boy Lost* (1949) by Marghanita Laski
No. 29 *The Making of a Marchioness* (1901) by Frances Hodgson Burnett
No. 30 *Kitchen Essays* (1922) by Agnes Jekyll
No. 31 *A House in the Country* (1944) by Jocelyn Playfair
No. 32 *The Carlyles at Home* (1965) by Thea Holme
No. 33 *The Far Cry* (1949) by Emma Smith

No. 34 *Minnie's Room: the Peacetime Stories of Mollie Panter-Downes 1947–65*
No. 35 *Greenery Street* (1925) by Denis Mackail
No. 36 *Lettice Delmer* (1958) by Susan Miles
No. 37 *The Runaway* (1872) by Elizabeth Anna Hart
No. 38 *Cheerful Weather for the Wedding* (1932) by Julia Strachey
No. 39 *Manja* (1939) by Anna Gmeyner
No. 40 *The Priory* (1939) by Dorothy Whipple
No. 41 *Hostages to Fortune* (1933) by Elizabeth Cambridge
No. 42 *The Blank Wall* (1947) by Elisabeth Sanxay Holding
No. 43 *The Wise Virgins* (1914) by Leonard Woolf
No. 44 *Tea with Mr Rochester* (1949) by Frances Towers
No. 45 *Good Food on the Aga* (1933) by Ambrose Heath
No. 46 *Miss Ranskill Comes Home* (1946) by Barbara Euphan Todd
No. 47 *The New House* (1936) by Lettice Cooper
No. 48 *The Casino* (1948) by Margaret Bonham
No. 49 *Bricks and Mortar* (1932) by Helen Ashton
No. 50 *The World that was Ours* (1967) by Hilda Bernstein
No. 51 *Operation Heartbreak* (1950) by Duff Cooper
No. 52 *The Village* (1952) by Marghanita Laski
No. 53 *Lady Rose and Mrs Memmary* (1937) by Ruby Ferguson
No. 54 *They Can't Ration These* (1940) by Vicomte de Mauduit
No. 55 *Flush* (1933) by Virginia Woolf
No. 56 *They Were Sisters* (1943) by Dorothy Whipple
No. 57 *The Hopkins Manuscript* (1939) by RC Sherriff
No. 58 *Hetty Dorval* (1947) by Ethel Wilson
No. 59 *There Were No Windows* (1944) by Norah Hoult
No. 60 *Doreen* (1946) by Barbara Noble
No. 61 *A London Child of the 1870s* (1934) by Molly Hughes
No. 62 *How to Run your Home without Help* (1949) by Kay Smallshaw
No. 63 *Princes in the Land* (1938) by Joanna Cannan
No. 64 *The Woman Novelist and Other Stories* (1946) by Diana Gardner
No. 65 *Alas, Poor Lady* (1937) by Rachel Ferguson
No. 66 *Gardener's Nightcap* (1938) by Muriel Stuart
No. 67 *The Fortnight in September* (1931) by RC Sherriff
No. 68 *The Expendable Man* (1963) by Dorothy B Hughes
No. 69 *Journal of Katherine Mansfield* (1927)
No. 70 *Plats du Jour* (1957) by Patience Gray and Primrose Boyd

No. 71 *The Shuttle* (1907) by Frances Hodgson Burnett
No. 72 *House-Bound* (1942) by Winifred Peck
No. 73 *The Young Pretenders* (1895) by Edith Henrietta Fowler
No. 74 *The Closed Door and Other Stories* by Dorothy Whipple
No. 75 *On the Other Side: Letters to my Children from Germany 1940–46* by Mathilde Wolff-Mönckeberg
No. 76 *The Crowded Street* (1924) by Winifred Holtby
No. 77 *Daddy's Gone A-Hunting* (1958) by Penelope Mortimer
No. 78 *A Very Great Profession: The Woman's Novel 1914–39* (1983) by Nicola Beauman
No. 79 *Round about a Pound a Week* (1913) by Maud Pember Reeves
No. 80 *The CountryHousewife's Book* (1934) by Lucy H Yates
No. 81 *Miss Buncle's Book* (1934) by DE Stevenson
No. 82 *Amours de Voyage* (1849) by Arthur Hugh Clough
No. 83 *Making Conversation* (1931) by Christine Longford
No. 84 *A New System of Domestic Cookery* (1806) by Mrs Rundell
No. 85 *High Wages* (1930) by Dorothy Whipple
No. 86 *To Bed with Grand Music* (1946) by 'Sarah Russell' (Marghanita Laski)
No. 87 *Dimanche and Other Stories* (1934–41) by Irène Némirovsky
No. 88 *Still Missing* (1981) by Beth Gutcheon
No. 89 *The Mystery of Mrs Blencarrow* (1890) by Mrs Oliphant
No. 90 *The Winds of Heaven* (1955) by Monica Dickens
No. 91 *Miss Buncle Married* (1936) by DE Stevenson
No. 92 *Midsummer Night in the Workhouse* (1962) by Diana Athill
No. 93 *The Sack of Bath* (1973) by Adam Fergusson
No. 94 *No Surrender* (1911) by Constance Maud
No. 95 *Greenbanks* (1932) by Dorothy Whipple
No. 96 *Dinners for Beginners* (1934) by Rachel and Margaret Ryan
No. 97 *Harriet* (1934) by Elizabeth Jenkins,
No. 98 *A Writer's Diary* (1953) by Virginia Woolf,
No. 99 *Patience* (1953) by John Coates
No. 100 *The Persephone Book of Short Stories*
No. 101 *Heat Lightning* (1932) by Helen Hull
No. 102 *The Exiles Return* (1958) by Elisabeth de Waal
No. 103 *The Squire* (1938) by Enid Bagnold
No. 104 *The Two Mrs Abbotts* (1943) by DE Stevenson
No. 105 *Diaryof a Provincial Lady* (1930) by EM Delafield
No. 106 *Into the Whirlwind* (1967) by Eugenia Ginzburg

No. 107 *Wilfred and Eileen* (1976) by Jonathan Smith
No. 108 *The Happy Tree* (1926) by Rosalind Murray
No. 109 *The Country Life Cookery Book* (1937) by Ambrose Heath
No. 110 *Because of the Lockwoods* (1949) by Dorothy Whipple
No. 111 *London War Notes* (1939–45) by Mollie Panter-Downes
No. 112 *Vain Shadow* (1963) by Jane Hervey
No. 113 *Greengates* (1936) by RC Sherriff
No. 114 *Gardeners' Choice* (1937) by Evelyn Dunbar & Charles Mahoney
No. 115 *Maman, What Are We Called Now?* (1957) by Jaqueline Mesnil-Amar
No. 116 *A Lady and Her Husband* (1914)by Amber Reeves
No. 117 *The Godwits Fly* (1938)by Robin Hyde
No. 118 *Every Good Deed and Other Stories* by Dorothy Whipple
No. 119 *Long Live Great Bardfield* (1942) by Tirzah Garwood
No. 120 *Madame Solario* (1956) by Gladys Huntington
No. 121 *Effi Briest* (1895) by Theodor Fontane
No. 122 *Earth and High Heaven* (1944) by Gwethalyn Graham
No. 123 *Emmeline* (1980) by Judith Rossner
No. 124 *The Journey Home and Other Stories* by Malachi Whitaker
No. 125 *Guard Your Daughters* (1953) by Diana Tutton
No. 126 *Despised and Rejected* (1918) by Rose Allatini
No. 127 *Young Anne* (1927) by Dorothy Whipple
No. 128 *Tory Heaven* (1948) by Marghanita Laski
No. 129 *The Call* (1924) by Edith Ayrton Zangwill
No. 130 *National Provincial* (1938) by Lettice Cooper
No. 131 *Milton Place* (1950) by Elisabeth de Waal
No. 132 *The Second Persephone Book of Short Stories*
No. 133 *Expiation* (1929) by Elizabeth von Arnim
No. 134 *A Room of One's Own* (1929) by Virginia Woolf
No. 135 *One Woman's Year* (1953) by Stella Martin Currey
No. 136 *The Oppermanns* (1933) by Lion Feuchtwanger
No. 137 *English Climate: Wartime Stories* (1940-46) by Sylvia Townsend Warner
No. 138 *The New Magdalen* (1873) by Wilkie Collins
No. 139 *Random Commentary* (1925-45) by Dorothy Whipple
No. 140 *The Rector's Daughter* (1924) by F M Mayor
No. 141 *The Deepening Stream* (1930) by Dorothy Canfield Fisher
No. 142 *As It Was* and *World Without End* (1926/31) by Helen Thoma
No. 143 *A Well Full of Leaves* (1943) by Elizabeth Myers

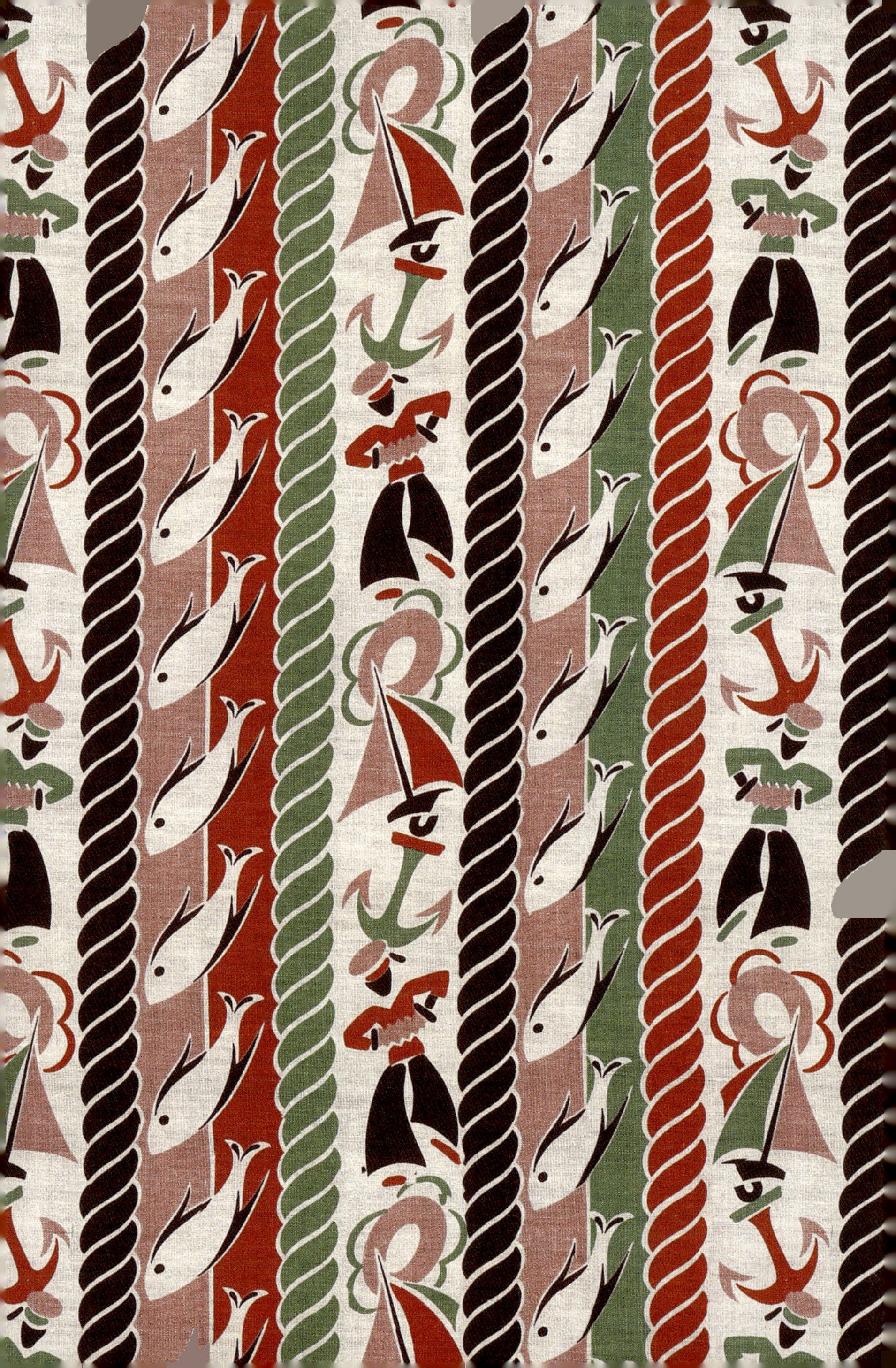